NEW GERMAN STUDIES MONOGRAPHS

D1628367

THE POETIC VISION OF

FRITZ USINGER

by

Christine R. Barker

NEW GERMAN STUDIES   GERMAN DEPARTMENT
HULL UNIVERSITY

1977

New German Studies Monographs

edited by

Rex Last & Alan Best

ISBN 0 85958 501 8

CONTENTS

ILLUSTRATIONS

THE POETIC VISION

OF

FRITZ USINGER

INTRODUCTION

Fritz Usinger was born on 5 March 1895 in Friedberg in
Hessen. He studied German, French and philosophy at the
universities of Munich, Heidelberg, and Gießen, where he
received his doctorate in 1921; he then taught until 1949
at secondary schools in Bingen, Offenbach am Main and
Bad Nauheim. Since his student days, a continuous stream
of poetry and essays has flowed from Usinger's pen, and
for fifteen years he was Vice-President of the Deutsche
Akademie für Sprache und Dichtung in Darmstadt; for many
years he has also been an active member of the Akademie
der Wissenschaften und der Literatur in Mainz, of the
PEN-Zentrum der Bundesrepublik, and a member of the Aca-
demia Goetheana at Sao Paolo in Brazil. He was awarded
the Georg-Büchner-Preis in 1946, the first to receive
this honour after the Second World War, and he also holds
the Goethe-Plakette and the Großes Bundesverdienstkreuz.
Since his retirement from teaching in 1949, Usinger has
established his home in the picturesque burgh of Friedberg,
where even now he continues to write with unabated vig-
our, producing poetry, translations, essays and aphorisms.
A volume of poems appeared in 1975 and yet another is
currently in the press; translations of some English
poems (including Donne, Keats and Swinburne) were published at Christmas 1975, and a new collection of aphorisms appeared in March 1976.

Usinger has dedicated his life to an unusual form of
literary 'engagement': he is convinced that the writer
has a 'missionary' purpose, and through his writings he
seeks to persuade mankind that the time has come for a
fundamental revision of values. Yet he remains non-
political, avoids social issues, and does not place un-
due emphasis on the situation of the individual in his
immediate environment. In a century in which literature
has become increasingly involved with social comment and
the rights of the individual, Usinger's work has so far
received scant attention. In academic circles his name
is familiar as a prominent member of the Darmstadt and

Mainz literary academies, as a translator of French Symbolist poetry, and, in the field of literary criticism, for his studies of Goethe, Hölderlin, Arp and others, yet Usinger's own major creative works have hitherto received only scant attention.

This study seeks to redress the balance by concentrating primarily on his major poetry, essays and aphorisms. An attempt has been made to preserve a chronological sequence where this does not conflict with the prime objective of presenting a picture of Usinger's complex yet unified Weltanschauung, which has evolved over decades of study and contemplation.

His work, both creative and critical, ranges over many different areas: not only literary topics, but also the visual arts, music, and beyond to mythology, mysticism, alchemy, mathematics, physics, biology, and cosmology. Each of these areas represents an aspect of man's vision of the universe and, taken together, they constitute a possible pathway bridging mankind and the infinite. While the arts offer scope to man's intuitive powers of perception, the sciences provide a factual basis upon which the intuition can work. Like Edgar Allan Poe, whom he so much admires, Usinger firmly believes that only by combining his reasoning faculties with his imaginative powers can man hope to penetrate the mysteries of creation.

Usinger's writings have a vast range of subject matter and span well over half a century, yet they have a unity of their own, namely, a constant concern to forge anew a direct relationship between the individual and the cosmos at large. Reasserting the central significance of spiritual values, Usinger endeavours to point to ways in which they can assist man to establish a new contact with the essential core of the universe, while at the same time tempering man's egocentricity. Usinger regards man's preoccupation with himself and with his own immediate interests as a distraction from his true function, namely, the utilisation of his intellectual and intuitive powers towards the attainment of a perfect world.

CHAPTER 1

MYSTICISM AND USINGER'S CONCEPTION OF GOD

While still a student, Usinger began his career as a lyric poet with contributions to the Expressionist periodical Die Dachstube, founded in 1915 by the fifteen-year-old Joseph Würth. These early poems were illustrated by original lithographs and wood and linocuts by Carl Gunschmann and Aloys Wach. Usinger also published a handful of essays in Die Dachstube which, like his poems, were concerned with mystical themes.

Der ewige Kampf, Usinger's first volume of poems, was published in September 1918 in a limited edition of 180 copies, with original lithographs by Carl Gunschmann. With the exception of the final quatrains, the collection consists entirely of sonnets, twenty-three in all. They are prefaced by a quotation from the Cherubinischer Wandersmann by the seventeenth-century mystic Angelus Silesius:

Der Abgrund meines Geists ruft immer mit Geschrei
Den Abgrund Gottes an: Sag, welcher tiefer sei? (1)

So it is not surprising that these poems, in conjunction with an essay in Die Dachstube entitled 'Mystik', demonstrate that mysticism was the dominant influence on the young Usinger.

The essence of mystical teaching is that all things are one and partake in a single, divine life in which individual being merges into a 'Universal Self' identifiable with God. God is not located in a heaven remote from man but dwells within the heart and mind of man - or can do so, once they have been sufficiently 'purged' to receive Him. In order to achieve this state, the unio mystica, man must be drained of all emotion and desire in order that the 'essential' self which remains might partake in the peace of God. Hence, to the mystic, the apparently negative term 'Abgrund' is in reality a positive concept, for the void shares the quality of infinity which is a characteristic of God. Hence, 'nothingness' becomes the highest

ideal. Elsewhere in the <u>Cherubinischer Wandersmann</u>
Silesius writes:

<u>Gott egreift man nicht</u>
Gott ist ein lauter Nichts, Ihn rührt kein Nun noch Hier:
Je mehr du nach Ihm greifst, je mehr entwird Er dir.
...
<u>Die Gottheit ist ein Nichts</u>
Die zarte Gottheit ist ein Nichts und Übernichts.(2)

The negative terminology applied to God reflects the fact
that the mystics considered the human mind inadequate to
describe an absolute which transcends all distinctions.
Man cannot know with any degree of certainty what God is,
only what He is not; any attempt to 'define' God limits Him
to human terms. This negative approach, the <u>via negativa</u>,
plays an important part in Usinger's later work.

According to mystical doctrine, the human self, or
'accidental' self, must be transformed in order to attain
a 'nothingness', a 'void', to equal the absence of self
which characterises God. Once this state has been achieved,
the identity between God and man is so complete that Silesius goes so far as to claim that God cannot live without
man:

Ich weiß, daß ohne mich Gott nicht ein Nu kann leben,
Werd ich zu nicht, er muß vom Not den Geist aufgeben. (3)

This claim that God's existence is as dependent on man as
man's is on God closely approaches the Expressionist concept of God as a projection of the human imagination, designed to fulfil a subjective need within man. In the essay
'Mystik', Usinger states

daß es der Mensch war, der Gott schuf, der ihn immer
wieder schafft, in sich, daß Gott erst durch des
Menschen Augen zum erstenmal die Welt, seine Welt sah ...
und sie lieben lernte. Alle große Mystik ist ein
Triumph des Ewig-Menschlichen. (4)

God was the initiator of the creation of the world, but only
through man's self-awareness and his consciousness of the

world about him does God assume any real significance.
'Der Mensch ist Vater; Gott des Menschen Kind', writes
Usinger elsewhere,(5) reversing the traditional relationship of God as Father and mankind as His children. Time
and space are concepts devised by man and only applicable
to earthly life; the mystics therefore do not feel bound to
regard the Creation as a specific temporal act on the part
of God, but consider it to be coeval with Him. The world,
they believe, is constantly being created anew.

Usinger also maintains that man's creation of God is
a continual process; he refers to man repeatedly creating
God from within his own heart:

O Gott, wie ist es schwer, dich immer wieder
Zu schaffen aus dem eigen schweren Herzen. (6)

'Schweren Herzen' implies that it is an emotional need on
the part of man which engenders God. With a skilful play
on words, Usinger goes on to state that man, finally overcome by a 'Schlaf der Erschöpfung', reflects upon the ad-
vantages of an animal existence bereft of consciousness,
unburdened with the responsibilities which man as a thinking being has to endure.

The quest for a new God had been an obsession in Germany
since the turn of the century and can be traced back to the
supposed 'destruction' of the Christian God by Nietzsche.
Mysticism was seized on by many as a substitute religion
because it is personal and non-institutional in nature.
Even Nietzsche could not achieve a complete rejection of
God: the compromise solution of a 'man-made' God fulfils
man's desire for a divine being while freeing him from the
shackles of organised religion. It is Silesius's emphasis
on the individual, together with the fact that he was a
poet, which gave him such a large following in the early
part of this century.

Silesius's preoccupation with the relationship between
God and man is also the predominant theme of Usinger's early
work. Usinger views the relationship in terms of a battle,
which the title 'Der ewige Kampf' denotes:

> Der Titel 'Der ewige Kampf' meint nicht anderes
> als den ewigen Kampf zwischen Mensch und Gott.
> Deshalb habe ich damals auch dem Buch als Motto
> jene zwei Zeilen von Angelus Silesius vorangestellt.(7)

Following the anthropocentricity of Expressionism, Usinger
places the main emphasis on man rather than on God. Far
from seeking to annihilate human characteristics, Usinger
endeavours to employ them as the basis for a new form of
belief. Der ewige Kampf depicts man's struggle to attain
a new conception of God founded on an initial faith in man:

> Du kannst zu mir in allen Kirchen beten.
> Ich bin dein Gott.(8)

Rather than the unio mystica, this poem expresses the necessity for dispensing with the old conception of God in
favour of new, more relevantly human ones; it advocates a
reliance on powers within the self rather than a dependence
on outside aid. The traditional Christian God is 'dead' and
man has been thrown back upon his own resources. He must
replace the old God with a 'human God' as described in Usinger's poem, not a trinity, simply a human being, yet endowed with the power to trample the old gods underfoot.
The power lies in man's imagination, which has the ability
to destroy the former image of God.

Unlike the God of the early mystics, who, it was believed,
sought out man as man sought God, Usinger's God does not
concern Himself with man, whom He has abandoned forever.
Usinger exhorts man to act on his own initiative, for no
divine hand of providence will come to his assistance; the
natural order of things cannot be disturbed for the sake of
man. Yet, although Usinger does not regard God as being
directly concerned with man, he does share with the mystics
a sense of the presence of the divine in the temporal. An
enduring attraction which mysticism holds for him is that
it does not regard God and the world, or spirit and matter,
as irreconcilable opposites, but teaches that God's eternal
and creative spirit is ever-present throughout the universe.
Like the mystics, Usinger regards Nature as an intermediary
between man and God, affording evidence of a divine spirit-

ual essence, but without the identification between God
and the material universe which characterises pantheism.
   In a later essay on mysticism, Usinger refers to the
'Signaturen-Lehre des Parazelsus und Böhmes ... die be-
sagt, daß die Dinge dieser Erde eine himmlische Schrift
sind, die es zu entziffern gilt'.(9) Usinger finds himself in agreement with the mystical view of the natural
world as the 'thinking out of God's thoughts';(10) he
himself reveals a similar conception of Nature when he
describes it as 'das wahre Wort Gottes'.(11) Every earthly object has within it a divine essence which is the
equivalent of the thoughts of God; each temporal creation
is thus endowed with a measure of spiritual immortality.
In this context, man has an important role to fulfil, for
it is his mind and imagination which discern and describe
these intimations of the divine. In the 'Vierzeiler'
which bring Der ewige Kampf to a close, Usinger views
man's position in the cosmos with greater objectivity
than in the sonnets which precede them and concedes that
man's 'reward' in earthly terms is commensurate with his
importance on earth, which, in contrast to that of other
'powers', is minimal. However, he places an entirely different value on man's spiritual worth:

   Des Menschen Lohn ist niemals ungemeiner,
   Als alle menschlichen Gewalten sind.
   Und dennoch ist im Himmel größer keiner:
   Der Mensch ist Vater, Gott des Menschen Kind.(12)

In terms of earthly power, man is greatly inferior to the
forces of Nature, but in 'heaven', in the spiritual realm,
his power is unsurpassed.
   Part of the appeal which mysticism holds for Usinger
lies in the strong element of paradox contained in its
teachings: God created man, as he did the rest of the
world, yet His own existence is determined by that of man;
God is present in Nature and in man, yet He has an existence as 'God' outside both. Usinger was later to crystall-
ise the problem in the following terms: 'Wenn der mensch-
liche Geist Götter schafft, bleibt immer noch die Frage:

wer schuf den Geist und seine Einbildungskraft?'(13) In a
letter, Usinger refers to his conception of God at the time
of his early work as 'seiend und nichtseiend zugleich.
Er ist nicht wahrnehmbar, aber dennoch muß seine Existenz
aus unzähligen Gründen angenommen werden.'(14) Despite
his assertion that God has abandoned man, the evidence
supplied by Nature's constant creativity leads Usinger to
the conclusion that God is still present in the cosmos,
or at least has left behind Him some of His creative powers.
Another reason for such a belief is the creativity which
Usinger experiences within himself in the form of poetic
inspiration. Employing a biblical image ('Ich bin der
Weg'), Usinger poses this question:

Bist du der Weg, wenn meine Hände tun,
was über deine wilden Stürme ziehlt:
Ich bin es selber nicht, der so befiehlt.(15)

Despite the self-assertion which accompanies the faith
that man controls God's fate, Usinger concedes that there
is some force outside himself which causes him to perform actions which he has not willed and whose purpose
he does not understand. It is clear that God, if indeed
these forces are to be identified with Him, has an existence entirely independent of man's rational conception of
Him.
   In Usinger's view, the poet has a special relationship
with the creative forces which testify to the existence of
some spiritual power in the world. The poet, who is
specially endowed with imaginative powers, evidently has
an important function to fulfil with regard to man's
imaginative conception of a divine presence in the universe. Poetry for Usinger is a form of 'mysticism': the
poet, like the mystic, is the recipient of a form of inspiration, often equated with ecstasy,(16) which he experiences as a communication with some extrinsic spiritual
force. The mystic, filled with a sense of the presence
of God, seeks to communicate this feeling to others, and
the poet, often inspired by a similar evangelical zeal,
endeavours to convey in words his vision of the divine.

God's most mysterious aspect is His self-sufficiency, which appears to conflict with the notion that His existence is dependent on man. Although man creates God from within himself, God already has some kind of existence which enables man to do this, and although man's image of God determines the way He appears, this 'creation' by man takes on a life of its own with which man can never fully come to terms:

> Ich denke den Gedanken niemals aus.
> Es ist das Lied, das sich von selber spinnt. (17)

Usinger returns to this theme time and again:

> Das Lied, das sich von selber singt,
> Die wunderbare Flöte,
> Die ohne Mund und Bläsen klingt. (18)

The flute plays 'unsterblich, unverwandt': unlike the mortals who 'create' Him, God is immortal and unchanging. The association between God and music assigns to God a divine essence of the same nature as the music of the spheres, which exists throughout all ages but which man interprets in different ways:

> Wohin ich sehe, stehst du am Beginn,
> ...
> Ich bin das Wort, doch du sein dunkler Sinn.
> So schließt sich überall das große Rund. (19)

Thus the Gott-Mensch relationship is a vicious circle: God is the beginning of all things, He is the meaning behind the terms imposed upon Him by man, yet without man's knowledge of Him, God's existence loses much of its significance. God is still accepted as the initiator of physical and spiritual existence, of Nature and of man, but a gulf has developed between God and man. Man cannot come to terms with God, but neither can God understand man who, like all earthly creatures, is constantly changing.

Another paradox of mysticism which constitutes a close and enduring bond with Usinger's work is the concept of

life within death. The mystic regards death as the lib-
erator of the true self:

> The corner-stone upon which the whole structure of
> mysticism rests is the gospel paradox that the self
> is saved by being lost, lives by dying.(20)

The mystic differentiates between physical death and
spiritual death: by the latter he means the death of the
self to the cares of the world. The self is gradually
purged of human will and emotions, which 'die' to be re-
placed by God's grace, that is, one's wilful or 'accidental' self makes room for the emergence of the 'essential'
self which then merges with God in a cosmic unity, the
unio mystica:

> Ich glaube keinen Tod; sterb ich gleich alle Stunden,
> So hab ich jedes Mal ein besser Leben funden.(21)

Physical death is no longer to be feared because it no
longer designates the end of existence: the cosmic unity
of which the purged self forms a part is immortal.

This positive acceptance of death, also advocated by
Schopenhauer and Nietzsche, is an important concept in
Usinger's work, but with Usinger the emphasis is on the
rejection of the notion of life and death as opposites -
a Goethean 'Stirb und werde!' - and is not concerned with
the 'emptying' of the ego and resultant fusion with the
cosmos and with God. Usinger applies the mystic's aspiration to the realm of art, hoping to attain a spiritual
level beyond the reach of worldly change and sorrow, and
even to the pain of final death. Suffering is affirmed
as a means towards this end; it tames the human will and
emotions, and from their death new spiritual awareness
is born as in Nature new life comes from decay.

In a poem entitled 'Ergebung', Usinger fuses 'death'
with 'joy' and 'renunciation', all of which mean more to
him than the traditional religious concepts conveyed by
the symbols 'Wein' and 'Brot':

Der mich mir schenkte, wird mir alles schenken:
Die Freudigkeit, Entsagung und den Tod,
Und alles dies ist mehr denn Wein und Brot.(22)

Usinger declares that the wishes which God denies are not
lost, but are collected together and purged from 'Zittern
und Hast' to form

ein tiefes Schauen,
das nichts begehrt und dennoch alles faßt,
dem Felsen, Wind und Wolken sich vertrauen,
das dauert, viele Ewigkeiten lang,
und groß hervorgeht aus dem Untergang.(23)

In the second stanza, this eternal, universal perception
is given as a final blessing - marking the insight which
comes with approaching death - but this does not mean
that the whole of life is wasted, waiting for death as
its sole fulfilment. Each work of art immortalises impressions of reality, whether or not the artist or poet
himself is fully aware of the import of his work. The
work of art is created as a lasting testimony to the
artist's perception of the eternal in the world and lives
on beyond his death. A poem or painting too is 'dead' in
the sense that it does not move and breathe, yet its meaning is a living one.

Usinger's poem 'Vor einer alten Pieta' is perhaps the
clearest expression of his interpretation of the entire
relationship between life, death, art and religion:

Uns hilft das Leben nicht. Uns hilft der Tod.
Denn dann erst wirken wir das Leben groß.(24)

It is death which gives meaning to life. The death of
Christ depicted in the pieta is the ultimate example of
this fact, for Christ came into the world specifically
in order to die, with the intention of thereby saving
man from his sins. It is this self-sacrifice on the
cross which is the entire foundation of Christianity, for,
without this, Christ would have retained the status of a
religious teacher and nothing more. The mystics regarded
Christ's suffering and death as an indication of the road

man must follow in order to inherit the eternal life He
'bought' for mankind. Silesius writes:

Gott selber, wenn er dir will leben, muß ersterben;
Wie, denkst du, ohne Tod sein Leben zu ererben?(25)

Christ's death serves as an example for the whole of mankind, for it demonstrates His self-sacrificing love. It
is not so much the manner of death which is important -
many were crucified - but the meaning attached to it. He
died for man, for a specific purpose, and His death was
not a finite action since He rose again from the dead.
This at least is the story which has affected the lives
of millions: whether the story is true or not, whether
Jesus of Nazareth actually was the Son of God, is to
Usinger irrelevant; the significance remains. Death
was a means to eternity for Jesus, and His martyrdom be-
came a universal symbol. It is the symbol of Christ's
death and Mary's faithfulness as depicted in the pieta
which is important for Usinger. He refers to the corpse
of Christ as 'noch von dem eignen Dulderblute rot'. The
image is still as vivid today as at the time of Christ's
death. For however long people may stand praying before
the pieta, says Usinger, it will remain alive. Even when
the actual figures depicted begin to be eaten by worms,
the spiritual beauty which the symbol contains will remain. Usinger is later to maintain that even when the
pages on which his words are written have disappeared,
the message itself will remain:

Das große Buch auf einem Fels gelegt,
...
Der Wind soll darin blättern,
Der Regen die Lettern verwaschen,
Die Sonne die Buchstaben bleichen,
Der Sturm die Seiten zerreißen
...
Das große Buch, auf einen Fels gelegt,
Wird nicht sterben, denn
...
Der Gestaltlose, der Nichts-Gott,

Der alles ist,
Er hat es gelesen.(26)

Mysticism is a philosophy concerned with the progression from the physical to the spiritual: the physical reality of man and of the world is 'purified' until it reaches a 'spiritual' essence which is undying. This principle is also the basis of Usinger's writing: he believes that everything in the world has an essential core which is immortal. This the poet seeks out and depicts in his work, stripping away the non-essential, transient aspects, which 'die' like the outer parts of a plant, leaving a 'seed' from which new growth is possible. Although Usinger soon ceases to regard the individual as the centre of experience, he continues to emphasise that an intuitive response to the world is the only means of establishing any real link with the fundamental truths of existence, for he has faith in the existence of a spiritual realm which can be attained by man in brief moments of unio mystica or poetic vision. Usinger's philosophical viewpoint is based on this 'mystical', intuitive perception of the core of existence, but is presented in orderly form and unified by the principle of the Logos; and it is to this subject that I now turn.

NOTES

1. Angelus Silesius, Sämtliche Poetische Werke, Munich, 1949, Vol.III, p.14.
2. Silesius, Sämtliche Poetische Werke, Vol.III, p.10 and 19
3. Silesius, Sämtliche Poetische Werke, Vol.III, p.8.
4. Die Dachstube, 4 (1918), Darmstadt, pp.246-7.
5. Usinger, Der ewige Kampf, Darmstadt, 1918, p.34.
6. Usinger, Sonette, Bad Nauheim, 1927, p.7.
7. Letter 49 (24.10.72). Correspondence quoted up to and including 29.12.74 is reproduced in Christine R. Barker, 'Fritz Usinger: Poet, Essayist and Critic. An investigation of his work.' Ph.D., Hull, 1975. The figures preceding the date refer to the letter number in the

thesis. Copies of all the correspondence have been lodged in the Brynmor Jones Library,University of Hull.

8. Usinger, Der ewige Kampf, p.16.
9. Usinger, Gesichter und Gesichte, Darmstadt, 1965, p.20.
10. Angelus Silesius, Selections from the Cherubinic Wanderer, translation and introduction by J. E. C. Flitch, London, 1932, p.87.
11. Usinger, Dichtung als Information, Mainz, 1970, p.16.
12. Usinger, Der ewige Kampf, p.34.
13. Usinger, Merkbücher, Mainz, 1976, p.66.
14. Letter 49 (24.10.72).
15. Usinger, Der ewige Kampf, p.11.
16. See C. R. Barker, 'Fritz Usinger: Poet, Essayist and Critic.' p.51f.
17. Usinger, Sonette, p.8.
18. Usinger, Sonette, p.27.
19. Usinger, Sonette, p.8.
20. Flitch, Selections from the Cherubinic Wanderer, p.80.
21. Silesius, Sämtliche Poetische Werke, Vol.III, p.10.
22. Usinger, Der ewige Kampf, p.28.
23. Usinger, Der ewige Kampf, p.28.
24. Usinger, Der ewige Kampf, p.7.
25. Silesius, Sämtliche Poetische Werke, Vol.III, p.10.
26. Usinger, Galaxis, Offenbach a.M., 1975, p.7.

CHAPTER 2

THE LOGOS AND THE LAW OF POLARITY

<u>Logos</u> is one of the oldest and most important concepts
in philosophical thought throughout history. It is a
Greek term meaning not only 'word', but also 'reason',
and 'wisdom'. The concept of the Logos began in Greek
thought around 560 BC with the Ephesian philosopher
Heraclitus, whose basic theory is that everything in
the world is in a state of flux, like a river whose
waters are continuously changing. But if that be so,
why is life not complete chaos? Heraclitus postulates
that the flux and change are not haphazard, but follow
an orderly pattern, and that this pattern is controlled
by the Logos, which is <u>the</u> principle of order under which
the universe continues to exist. He believes there to be
a purpose in all life, not only in the physical world,
but in everything which happens, the Logos being the power
governing this purpose. He also believes the Logos to be
present in the mind of man as the power which enables us
to think and reason, to recognise the truth when we see
it, and to judge between right and wrong. The Logos
cannot be assessed in terms of the human mind alone,
since this is only a minute part of its domain, but it
is equivalent to the mind of God, controlling the world
and man. The idea of the Logos developed in Stoic thought.
The Stoics were amazed at the order of the world and, like
Heraclitus, attributed to the Logos the power which puts
meaning into the world, creating order instead of chaos
and pervading all things. The Logos is envisaged as a
kind of universal Reason which resides in the individual
and in the universe at large.
    The close association which exists between the Logos
and the Word was developed by the Jews. To the Jew, a
word was far more than a mere sound: it was something
which had an active and independent·existence and which,
once spoken, had an autonomous power. Hence the importance of a blessing in the Old Testament: once Isaac has

given Jacob his blessing instead of Esau, he cannot re-
tract it. The Word also has the power of creation. The
word of God is the power which creates the whole world -
in Genesis, each part of the creation of the world is
preceded by 'And God said ...', or, in the thirtieth
Psalm: 'By the word of God were the heavens made'. In
later Jewish history, 'the Word of God' was used as a
euphemism for God Himself. The Alexandrian Jew Philo
studied both Jewish and Greek thought and synthesised the
concept of the Logos, which he considered to be the old-
est thing in the world, the thought of God stamped upon
the universe, an object of eternal existence with a
creative power, a life-giving function, which constitutes
an intermediary between the world and God. It was because logos was a conception familiar to Jewish and
Greek peoples alike that St John used 'The Word' as a
synonym for Christ as the embodiment of the Logos, the
Word made flesh.

The theme of 'das Wort', or the Logos, is a central
part of Usinger's work, from his earliest poetry up to
the present day. As a unifying and omnipresent power, it
represents a logical step from the mystical, law-giving,
spiritual 'God', for his basic conception of the Logos
is like that formed by Herclitus, that is, as a controlling force lending form and order to a continually changing
universe - a universe which, without the presence of the
Logos, would be utter chaos. Some parts of the universe
may appear to be chaos or darkness, but even here the
Logos is to be found, unseen by human eyes:

> Der Begriff des Chaos ist anthropomorph. Vom
> Kosmos aus gesehen gibt es kein Chaos, sondern nur
> verschiedene Existenzstufen. Wo die geringste Form
> von Sein ist, ist auch schon eine Ordnung. Jede
> Form des Seins, auch die unterste, hat ihre Art
> von Ordnung. Sobald irgendeine Form von Sein in
> Erscheinung tritt, manifestiert sich eine Art von
> Ordnung. 'Chaos' ist nur eine Art von minderer,
> einfacherer Ordnung. Kosmos ist eine Form von
> höherer, komplizierterer Ordnung.(1)

The Logos, with its life-giving and ordering powers
is present in every atom, for it is the criterion of existence: 'Der Logos ist die gesetzliche Form schlechthin, bis
in die kleinsten Teile hinein. Ohne Logos gäbe es über-
haupt kein Sein'.(2) The Logos bestows life and meaning;
its creative powers know no limits but are found everywhere, in form, in chaos, in every part of every thing.

In Usinger's earlier works, the concept of 'The Word'
is equated with God, and still retains many of the associations of traditional Christianity. The poem 'Das Wort'
in Der ewige Kampf, for example, begins with these words:

O Gott, du dunkles Wort, darum wir kreisen.(3)

The Word here is the means by which God reveals Himself
directly to man, the words of the prophets and of Christ.
As Usinger's appreciation of Nature increases, however,
he sees God revealed in this too, and his concept of
'The Word' expands to include the voices of Nature - the
sound of water, for example, or the rustling of grass and
leaves - which often seem more real and closer to the
divine essence than does the human word: 'Das bewußte
Wort ist vielleicht nur ein kleiner Teil des Worts, jener
Wortwelt, die sich durch alles Seiende und vielleicht
auch sogar durch alles Nicht-Seiende hindurchzieht.'(4)
The Logos is an impersonal, divine principle, whose life-
giving and ordering forces are found in all of creation
and whose spirit endures the disappearance of its individual manifestations, whether these be natural forms or
abstract ideas. In the poem 'Das Wort' in Sonette Usinger
writes:

Es wird das Wort nicht mit der Welt vergehen.
Durch Tosen tönt die Stimme ungebrochen,
Aus Wogen tauchend mit erneutem Schalle.

The world may change or even perish, but the Word lasts
forever. Not only can it endure the world's transience,
it can even hold the gods in check:

Es hält das Wort die Götter selbst in Schwebe.
So ist der Geist noch fest, wenn auch das Treue
Hingeht und weint und weiß nicht, wie es lebe.(5)

The Logos appears in various forms in all material and
spiritual life, and the gods as well as man are subordinate to its power. At a later date Usinger writes of the
Greek gods: 'Natürlich hatten alle diese Götter eine
Logos-Beziehung. Sie waren ja alle nur Teilkräfte des
Logos.'(6) The immortality of the Word is, together with
its universality, the major aspect of the Logos-theme
for Usinger and is referred to constantly throughout his
works. This immortality is manifested in the natural
world by the apparent changelessness of Nature's overall
structure, despite the decay of individual elements, and,
in symbolic form, in art and mythology.

The first of Usinger's works to really explore the
theme of the Logos is the collection entitled Das Wort,
which also marks the beginning of a coherent development
in Usinger's philosophy. Usinger comments: 'Dieses Ge-
dichtwerk Das Wort (1931) spricht auf eine sehr zarte und
ahnende Weise von der Geburt des Worts in der Welt.'(7)
It is ironic that a collection dealing with the 'birth of
the Logos in the world' should open with a poem entitled
'Ballade vom jüngsten Gericht', which depicts the destruction of the earth. The paradox, however, is of life within
death, encountered in the previous chapter, for spirit is
more enduring than matter and the earth's destruction is
accompanied by the reunification of the Word, whose powers of endurance are great enough to resist even the end
of the world. The poem begins with an imprecise statement -

> Ein Tag ist angebrochen,
> Der leuchtet wunderbar (8)

- which implies that the significance of this particular
day is at first unknown. Stanza three is more specific:
'Der Tag ist angebrochen, / Er leuchtet allem Land.'
'Ein Tag' has become 'der Tag' and the light does not
simply 'shine' but illuminates the earth - it has a purpose. The disappearance of all life is described very
impersonally:

> Es bricht die harte Krume.
> Es kollert. Erde grollt.

Usinger is careful to point out that the beautiful and the
ugly vanish together, and a reference to the 'böser Wurm'
eliminates the distinction between the beginning and end
of time – the snake which was there in the Garden of Eden
is still there at the world's end. Most important of all
is the reunification of all language – the rumbling of the
earthquake mingles with whispers and sighs:

> Wort will mit Wort sich mischen,
> Wo keines mehr sich weiß.

All sounds will again become one Word, without distinction
and without individuality. Self-awareness emanates from
a consciousness that one is not part of the whole, and as
the physical forms of creation perish, their spirit is
united in a harmony which allows of no individuality.

Humanity too must perish – the human mouth, senses and
eyes are all useless now. Mankind still awaits the traditional coming of God, with silver clouds of angels' wings:

> Des weißen Aases Feier,
> Dies ist der Tag gelobt:
> Komm, Gott, durch Wolkenschleier,
> Vom Engel-Silbermeer umtobt. (9)

This stanza occurs twice: everyone awaits the promised
salvation, both the innocent and the guilty wait – or the
'rein und schuldig' could mean that everyone is half-
innocent and half-guilty. But there is no sound of trump-
ets or of angels' wings. In the growing darkness all that
comes is: 'Ein Wind, ein kleiner Wind'. God, or the Logos,
is often the 'still, small voice' for Usinger, to be
found in the simple things in life, not a glorious spect-
acle. Even in Der ewige Kampf, Usinger is certain that
God's coming will not be as expected, although its exact
nature is not clear to him. He is now convinced that the
'divine' is already present in the world, concealed in the
'voices' of Nature. The final two stanzas sum up Usinger's
attitude:

Die Sonnen Gottes tragen
Nicht Engelsangesicht.
Die Sonnen Gottes fragen
Nach einem Menschen nicht.

Die Sonnen Gottes gehen
Einen uralten Gang.
Sie können Gott nicht sehen
Und sind doch sein Gesang. (10)

God's messengers do not look like angels, nor do they
carry out their expected function, namely, of saving man.
On the contrary, they have no concern with man, but are
as remote as Hölderlin's gods. All traces of an Expressionist anthropocentric universe have now vanished from
Usinger's work. 'Die Sonnen Gottes' are not sent specifically for man, they are just a part of the world which
has been in existence for years and will continue to exist -
with or without man. They cannot see God, for they are
part of Him. Usinger is trying to re-establish a similar
kind of unity or harmony for man by referring him back to
the unifying presence of the Logos in creation; this he
regards as far more worthwhile than any dependence on a
future solution or 'Day of Judgement'.

The poem 'Vox Coelestis' develops the idea of the perm-
anence of the Word. It is more personal than 'Ballade
vom jüngsten Gericht'; Usinger speaks from his own point
of view:

So durch die Jahre stürzend, im Gefäll
Der Zeiten abwärts, ob ich sinke, schwimme,
Bei Bildern, wechselnd träge oder schnell,
Ich höre stets die tiefe Orgelstimme. (11)

Usinger retains the symbol of the sound of the organ for
the vox coelestis, the 'heavenly' or immortal voice of
the Logos, throughout his work. He declares that it is
'eine mystische Idee' which attracts him to the organ,
for he regards it as the most powerful intermediary between the human and the divine.(12) The organ is composed
of earthly materials and played by a human agent, yet the

sound it gives forth is to Usinger of an unearthly splend-
our, as if the whole world has burst into song: 'das
Elementarische wird in der Orgel erhöht und fängt selbst
an zu singen'.(13) Although the divine has no language of
its own, Usinger considers organ-music to be the closest
approximation to a universal and immortal song, striking
at the innermost chords of the universe which are beyond
man's reach. The sound is not loud, yet it penetrates
everything, even man's dreams: 'kaum hörbar Summen, doch
durch alles dringend'.(14) Whatever changes may occur
in the fortunes of the individual, the Logos remains unaltered. Whether Usinger tries to 'embrace' the sound or
flees from it to the solace of human society, it remains
'unfaßbar'. Man has no influence at all over the voice;
he cannot even escape from it.

The term 'Abgrund' encountered in Der ewige Kampf recurs throughout Usinger's work, denoting a part of the
universe which to man appears as void, but which in reality has a law and meaning of its own. In a later poem,
Usinger refers to the 'Abgrund' as the home of the Logos:

> Seine Wohnungen sind
> Im Unfindbaren, in den
> Abgründen hinter dem Funken Canopus,
> Wo die Unsichtbarkeit wohnt. (15)

Those manifestations of the Logos which are perceptible
to the human senses afford only an intimation of its total
reality, for it is also to be found in invisible, formless
regions which are completely outside man's experience:

> Wenn auch der Logos in die Welt ergossen ist, wir
> erfassen ihn nicht, denn zwischen ihm und uns liegt
> brennend das - auch göttliche - 'Aorgische', um mit
> Hölderlin zu reden, das ungeheure Gestaltlos-
> Lebendige.(16)

Human thought and philosophy have their limits, but not
so the Logos:

> Das Denken denkt seine Grenzen,
> Aber der Logos hat die Flügel eines
> Erzengels und schwingt sich,
> Wohin er will. (17)

Not only does the Logos reside within all forms of existence, it is also the meaning which is imposed upon them:

> Das Wort ist das große, weltordnende Prinzip. Es ist
> über den Dingen, in den Dingen und ebenso alles das,
> was der Mensch als geistige Perspektive den Erschein-
> ungen leiht. (18)

This spiritual dimension of the Logos may be sensed in-
tuitively, but it cannot be comprehended, for it surpasses
the bounds of human logic. Usinger believes that man is
sometimes granted a moment of vision corresponding to the
unio mystica when, for a short time, he is able to parti-
cipate in Nature's spiritual eternity.

In order to achieve this intuitive contact with the
Logos, which represents the ordered plan of the universe,
man must humbly accept his subordinate position:

> Glaube mir, ich weiß zu dienen!
> Einem großen Schicksal untertan. (19)

Usinger often equates 'Schicksal' with 'Logos' as denoting
universal laws which man must obey without understanding
them. There is no suggestion of active intervention in
the affairs of man such as is contained in the Greek concept of Fate. Usinger's mind accepts the notion of the
Logos more readily than that of the Christian God, and he
willingly considers himself as part of the general pattern
of a universe where even the smallest part of creation
has a unique value:

> Trag das Kleine achtsam auf dem Finger!
> Niemals weißt du, wenn es fällt,
> Ob es Perlen wert ist, ob geringer -
> Oder eine Welt.
>
> So beschreiten wir das Wunderbare,
> Ohne es zu sehen. (20)

The closest communication with the Logos is experienced
against a simple and tranquil natural background, where
man can escape from the distractions of a world of comm-
erce and industry. Yet man often overlooks the miracles
of creation because he never takes the time to stop and
consider them: 'Still, ganz still, und horch!'(21) - such
is the exhortation which Usinger is to repeat time and
again in his work, for an undemanding attitude of calm
acceptance will more often reveal the true value of a
phenomenon than man's faculties of reason.

Although the term 'logic' is derived from _logos_, human
intelligence is but a minute fraction of the 'universal
intelligence' represented by the Logos, just as human
language is one minute part of the language of Nature:

> Der menschliche Verstand ist nur ein winziger
> Ausschnitt des Welt-Logos. Der wichtigste Unter-
> schied zwischen dem menschlichen Verstand und dem
> Welt-Logos besteht darin, daβ der Welt-Logos unend-
> lich viel umfassender ist, nämlich auch alle Regionen
> des Nicht-Logischen umfaβt.(22)

What human logic categorises as 'das Kleine' may be 'eine
Welt' if judged by other criteria, by the alogical criteria
of the 'Welt-Logos'.

Despite the fact that the human word, both spoken and
written, represents only a tiny part of the Logos and
is often inadequate as an expression of its mysteries,
Usinger believes the poet can perform an invaluable function
by interpreting the manifestations of the Logos in Nature
and transforming them into words:

> Gottes Sprache ist die Schöpfung der Materie mit
> ihren wortlosen Ur-Lauten. Nur durch den Menschen
> tönt Gottes Sprache in Worten.(23)

The poet, as one who is granted special insight into the
various testimonies of the Logos in the world, enables mankind to share his insight by translating it into human
language. In addition, he adds a further dimension to
the Logos, one whose powers of endurance are equal, if

not superior, to its manifestations in the natural world.

A poem from Das Wort, 'Man wird dich nicht vergessen', summarises Usinger's view of the poet's position in the world. The phrase which forms the title is repeated five times in the course of the poem, at irregular intervals, often standing in antithesis to the preceding statement, and on four occasions prefaced by 'aber'. The entire poem, in fact, is constituted of antithetical statements, a favourite device of Usinger's:

> Viele sahen dich, aber es sah dich keiner.
> Du bist gezeichnet und auserwählt.
> Sie gehen an dir vorbei, ohne dich anzusehen.
> Aber man wird dich nicht vergessen.(24)

While the rest of mankind is too preoccupied with the bustle of everyday life to perceive the Logos, or listen to the poet, the latter devotes himself to the task of immortalising his impressions of external reality. Like Goethe's 'Urbilder', the Logos incorporates the essential features of each life-form, and the poet translates the almost imperceptible signs of eternal meaning into human terms, thus clothing in words a realm which must otherwise remain silent.

It is the task of the poet to convey in language which man can comprehend not only the sense of unity and beauty which he perceives in the world, but also the threat of chaos:

> Unsichtbare Hände würgen, zerrn,
> Und das Chaos stürzt mit schwarzem Schwall
> In das Reich des Herrn.(25)

The forces of chaos are ever-present and must be acknowledged if they are to be resisted at all. Usinger comes to believe that the world exists as a polarity of order and chaos, represented here by the 'Reich des Herrn' and 'Chaos' respectively. The Logos is present even in chaos, not in sufficient force to give a picture of order, but in embryonic form it pervades each individual particle of which that chaos is composed:

> Form ist immer, auch im Chaos, schon in der ursprüng-
> lichsten plasmatischen Fügung. Schon das Gas-Atom
> hat eine 'unendlich' komplizierte Form. Jede Welle,
> jede Schwingung, jeder Strahl ist Form. Nur das
> Nichts ist ohne Form, aber gerade das Nichts gibt
> es nicht.(26)

The apparent absence of meaning and order is attributed
by Usinger to man's faulty powers of perception, never
to the world itself. Like the chaos which is said to have
preceded the initial creation of the world, Usinger believes that any state of chaos can be dispelled, if its
potential towards order is encouraged to develop.

The Weltanschauung which gradually emerges from
Usinger's work of the 'thirties constitutes a system
of tension between 'positive' and 'negative' elements
such that shifts in the one direction are ultimately
balanced by corresponding changes in the other, so that
the totality remains unaltered, with the Logos as the
unifying factor. This system, which Usinger summarises
as the 'Ja und Nein der Welt',(27) is also called the
Two Contraries (the Chinese Yin-Yang). This doctrine,
whatever its origins, may be found under various names
in the mythological systems of all ancient civilisations
and in modern science in the form of the positive and
negative attributes in electricity.(28) According to
it, the continued existence of the world is dependent
on the interaction between these two attributes, which
are in state of polarity rather than direct opposition.
Like the early philosophers, Usinger believes that the
Two Contraries share the same source, and much of his
subsequent work is concerned with his seeking to come
to terms with the 'negative' aspect of life.

The basic principle of the world as a polarity of
positive and negative forces which have a common source
comes into Usinger's philosophy by way of Heraclitus
and the medieval philosopher Nicholas of Cusa. Heraclitus writes in terms of an 'attunement of opposite
tensions, like that of the bow and the lyre'.(29) This
relates to his theory of strife which he regards as

essential for the continued existence of the universe:
'We must know that war is common to all and strife is
justice, and that all things come into being and pass away
through strife'.(30) Perpetual strife is the normal state,
for in strife opposites come together to generate that
energy which is the life-force sustaining the universe.
This energy is in a state of flux (as demonstrated in the
celebrated river-image employed by Heraclitus), which is
harmony through diversity: harmony because the energy is
always present, diversity because the forms to which it
gives rise are ever changing.

Cardinal Nicholas of Cusa (1401-1464) developed the
concept of the coincidentia oppositorum. He believed that
there were two ways of viewing the universe, 'intellectual-
iter' and 'rationaliter'. His coincidence of opposites
accounts for intellectual knowledge and the principle of
contradiction for rational knowledge. Intelligence sees
the unity behind contraries which reason contrasts and
declares to be mutually exclusive. So the Cardinal's definition of 'intelligence' corresponds to the intuitive,
non-rational powers of man's mind. These views (expressed
primarily in his De doctra ignorantia of 1440) have much
in common with the Neo-Platonists, in particular with the
doctrine of Proclus, with whose works Nicholas was well
acquainted. The Neo-Platonists believed in a hierarchy
of beings, from angels or intelligences at one end of the
scale to the lower spirits at the other. Proclus seeks to
show how each degree in the hierarchy of living beings contains the fullness of reality but reveals it from a different angle. In the 'One', all things are indistinct; in
'Intelligence' they interpenetrate, because of an intuitive
vision which sees all things in each thing; in 'Soul' they
are no longer bound by anything but the bonds of discursive
reason, that is, man's rationality; and in the world, each
object simply exists in its own right without the links
provided by man's varying degrees of perception. Thus the
intellectual knowledge and rational knowledge which
Nicholas of Cusa speaks of correspond to Intelligence
and Soul in the hierarchy which Proclus describes.

'Intellectual' or 'intuitive' knowledge helps to restore
unity to all the disparate elements of the world.

The parallels with Usinger's views are evident: he too
envisages knowledge as a means to unity and also conceives
of various stages of knowledge, beginning with the analytic-
al investigation of existing phenomena, then proceeding to
rational evaluation, and finally to an intuitive awareness
of correspondences beyond the logical. Usinger speaks of
his indebtedness to Nicholas of Cusa in a letter:

> Das häufige Vorkommen von 'aber' und 'doch' hängt
> mit einem tiefen Wesenszug meiner Dichtung und
> Weltanschauung zusammen, nämlich mit dem, was der
> mittelalterliche Philosoph Nickolaus von Kues die
> coincidentia oppositorium, die Einheit der Gegen-
> sätze, nannte. Diese tiefe Verbundenheit von Hell
> und Dunkel, Gut und Böse, Himmel und Hölle, zieht
> sich durch mein ganzes Lebenswerk hindurch.(31)

There are many ways in which negative forces can have
positive results - for example, as a means of contrast,
through which the true value of perfection and order
can be clearly perceived in opposition to life's apparent
meaninglessness and imperfection. Similarly, an awareness of the negative side of life can incite man to
strive for the creation of positive values where none
exist - in works of art, for example. Nature, it has
often been pointed out, depends upon forces of decay
and destruction for the continued production of new life
and beauty.

However, Usinger does not simply regard the negative
aspects of the world as a contrast by which the positive
may be perceived, nor does he grudgingly accept them as
necessary for the continued existence of the world. In
line with his constant consciousness of the universe as
a whole, he is able to interpret the majority of negative aspects in a positive and formative sense.

The opening words of <u>Genesis</u> state that God made light
out of darkness and then separated the two - implying
that they were originally one. He did not transform

all darkness into light, but allowed both to exist –
similarly with the negative forces which darkness symbolises. Usinger's 'God', like the God in _Faust_, uses the
forces of evil as well as those of good:

> Was sucht ihr mich in der
> Goldenen Wolke?
> ...
> In blutigem Panzer kommt
> Zu Zeiten der Gott
> ...
> Hier ist zu
> Fürchten nicht, sondern
> Dazusein, zu gehen in den
> Feurigen Ofen und zu
> Singen aus Flammen. Denn
> Unteilhaft ist alles.(32)

Although the basic unity of creation is not readily visible
to man, Usinger believes that without a system of polarity
to maintain a state of order in the universe, the world
would revert to the chaos which preceded the initial sep-
aration of darkness and light:

> Löse
> Die Freuden nicht heraus, du
> Stürbest im Chaos. Lieber
> Lasse den Dämon auf dem
> Stuhle des Herrn, denn
> Eingesetzt ist er und soll dein
> Meister sein.(33)

One day, says Usinger, the demon will assume the features
of an angel and allow us to hope that the earth is not
irrevocably lost. No state is permanent, and even the
darkest hours are not without hope.

In his early poetry, where mankind is still the criterion by which all events are judged, 'evil' is accorded
a purpose which has direct bearing on the relationship
between God and man: it has an admonitory function, namely,
to teach man that he has no right to expect unalloyed

happiness; it reminds man that he is not in complete control of his own destiny; and it serves as a test for man's
faith. As Usinger's awareness of the limitless expanse
of the cosmos evolves, and with this the realisation that
human life and values play a minute role in the universe
as a whole, he no longer considers it necessary to explain
life's negative side as relating directly to man. If it
seems incomprehensible to man that creatures and events
which are inimical to all human and plant life should be
accorded a place in the world, Usinger maintains that this
is because man is caught in a web of anthropocentricity.

The whole problem of good and evil, positive and negative, appearance and reality, as they are manifested in
earthly existence is examined by Usinger in a series of
sestinas in Die Geheimnisse (1937). Usinger adopts this
old Italian poetic form as appropriate to the complex yet
symmetrical relationship which he perceives in the laws
dominating man's place in creation. Each sestina has six
stanzas whose six lines share the same rhyme-scheme and
some of the same rhyme-words. Usinger probes every aspect of the relationship between 'imperfect' man and a
perfect and infinite God, often focussing the subtleties
of key issues in the rhyme-words. The central poem of
these 'Sestinen von Sein und Schein' is the 'Sestine der
Unsagbarkeit' which Usinger summarises in these words:

> Sie besagt, daß das, was in der Welt als Abfall
> von Gott erscheint (Luzifer) notwendig ist, da ohne
> Abfall überhaupt keine Welt entstehen und bestehen
> kann. (34)

In a letter, Usinger also designates this poem as the
transition point from the theological stand of his earlier
work to that of his mature work, which he describes as
'naturphilosophisch'. (35) There remains no vestige of
a personal relationship between God and man in Usinger's
work, for God now exists only as an impersonal creative
principle whose meaning, if inexpressible, is to be
found in every part of the universe. The problem, for
Usinger, is no longer primarily a moral one - God's

condonation of evil - but extends beyond the confines of
human morality to the amoral realm of Nature as a whole.
The mysteries of creation need to be comprehended, not in
terms of Christianity, but as natural laws appertaining
to the whole of existence.

From _Die Geheimnisse_ onwards, negative prefixes like
the 'un-' which occurs in three of the sestinas - 'Unsagbarkeit', 'Unwiederbringlichkeit' and 'Unvollendbarkeit' -
are characteristic of Usinger's poetry. In a letter,
Usinger relates the negative elements in his vocabulary
to the negative theology of the Middle Ages, to which
reference was made in Chapter One, clarifying at the same
time its relationship to the Logos and his revised conception of God:

> Mit diesem Logos-Kern der Welt hängt auch das häufige
> Vorkommen von Verneinungs-Wörten in meinen Texten
> zusammen, wie etwa die Wörter 'nicht', 'kein',
> 'niemand', oder wie der häufige Gebrauch der vernein-
> enden Vorsilben 'un-' oder auch 'ur-', das ja häufig
> mit der Silbe 'un-' nahe verwandt ist. Es gab im
> Mittelalter eine sogenannte negative Theologie.
> Weil man über Gott nichts an sachlichen Bestimmungen
> aussagen konnte, beschränkte man sich auf Aussagen,
> die alles das bezeichneten, was er nicht sei. Man
> versuchte also eine Art Einkreisung von der Negation
> her. Genau das Gleiche finden Sie bei mir. Nur ist
> es bei mir nicht Gott, von dem unmittelbar die Rede
> ist, sondern das Universum, was vielleicht nur ein
> anderes Wort für Gott ist. Auch dieses Universum
> besteht im wesentlichen aus unsagbaren oder unvor-
> stellbaren Qualitäten.(36)

It was noted earlier that Usinger often describes the
Logos in the vaguest of terms: it is a 'kaum hörbar
Summen',(37) it is 'unfaßbar', and its home is 'im
Unfindbaren, in den Abgründen hinter dem Funken Canopus,
wo die Unsichtbarkeit wohnt.'(38) Usinger approaches the
Logos, as the unifying and creative force in the uni-
verse, in the same way that the mystics of the Middle

Ages approached God. Yet the fact that the negative terms
which he employs can exist at all implies that somewhere
there is a standard of perfection against which they can
be measured.

Negative aspects are to be found in various realms of
experience, including that of the imagination. Several
of the poems in Irdisches Gedicht (1927) are concerned
with the transformation of the everyday into nightmare
experiences, which vanish again as daylight returns. This
theme recurs in Die Geheimnisse, where particular emphasis
is placed upon the contrast between day-time and night-
time appearances:

> Die ihr mir am Blute zehret
> Nächtens schwer auf meiner Brust,
> Daß der Arm vergeblich wehret
> Eurer möderischen Lust:
>
> Ach, ihr seid bei Tageslicht
> Herrlich. Euer Lippenbogen
> In dem marmornen Gesicht
> Ist von einem Gott gezogen.(39)

The vampires' features assume an almost divine tranquility in the daylight as they revert to their normal role
of marble statues. The duality in this case is a con-
sequence of the world of 'Schein' which man inhabits:
this causes external phenomena to adopt contrasting and
deceptive appearances in accordance with the subjective
mood of the observer. For some, the deception of appearances furnishes proof of the senselessness of man's existence, where not even visual evidence can be believed, but
Usinger accepts it as part of a world of changes. The
changes which take place in man's imagination stand as a
corollary to natural changes, as a result of which night
follows day and spring follows winter: they are equally
a mixture of positive and negative.

Usinger believes that a positive evaluation even of
the most inexplicable features of life is the only means
of countering the forces of destruction at work in the
universe. Even despair must be not only accepted, but

also transformed into something positive:

> Verloren ist, wer nur den Himmel will.
> Ich nehme alle Höllen hinzu mit ihren Feuern,
> ...
> Wer rettet mich?
> Niemand rettet mich, auch du nicht,
> Nur das Ja, das ich selber zu der Verzweiflung spreche.
> In deinem Kuß liegt die Hölle neben dem Himmel.
> Wer will sie trennen?
> Ich muß sie beide lieben
> Und das Verhängnis in Gold verwandeln.(40)

In personal relationships, as in all else, the sorrow must be taken along with the joy and itself transformed into a form of happiness. In another poem of the series 'Himmel und Hölle', from which the above extract is taken, Usinger speaks of 'die Gleichheit von Glück und Unglück':

> Versuche nicht, sie zu trennen!
> Es wird dir nie gelingen.
> Du müßtest denn ein Gott sein
> Und die Welt auflösen
> In eine Wolke kosmischen Staubes,
> Die nichts mehr weiß von Glück und Unglück.
> ...
> Die Gleichheit von Glück und Unglück,
> Sie ist das höchste Arcanum, das Heil-Wissen
> Gegen ein Meer des Unheils,
> Dem kein Mensch zu widerstehen vermag.(41)

The 'Wolke kosmischen Staubes' is the equivalent of 'chaos', which will result if the close relationship which exists between the positive and negative poles is severed. 'Verzweiflung' and 'Unglück', like the concept of the 'Abgrund', are negative concepts with 'positive' connotations, since the effort required to overcome them itself constitutes a major positive force. While the rest of creation has no choice but to submit to whatever force is prevalent at the time, mankind must assert his free-will to prevent the negative elements from gaining the upper hand, for once the

'Meer des Unheils' has gained full control, it will be too
late. Man is the only creature with consciousness and
therefore the only living being capable of guiding the
development of the world. Usinger emphasises the need
for love - with its aid, the dual forces of the world,
the positive and negative, the ideal and real, can work
together:

> Da ihm im Traum erscheint das höchste Reine,
> Mag manchem wohl sein Herz so zage klingen.
> Daß trüber Stoff sich klarstem Bilde eine,
> Mit welchem Flügeln mag man das erschwingen?
>
> Es ist ein Doppelreich, aus dem wir stammen:
> Aus einem Vater-, einem Mutterlande.
> Einfachste Liebe füge sie zusammen,
> Dann leben sie im höchsten Einverstande.(42)

Love unites the disparate elements without needing to
understand precisely how they are connected. For Usinger,
'Logos' and 'Liebe' are practically synonymous terms because they share the ability to lend meaning and order to
all aspects of life. Love is a cosmic phenomenon, as universal as the Logos, or at least capable of being so. Unlike the Logos, love has special associations with mankind,
and it is man who is responsible for extending the range
of its powers. The poet can do this through his works.
Usinger often refers to the poet as 'der Liebende', some-
one who loves the world despite its many faults and finds
value and meaning everywhere.
Yet, the awesome aspects of the 'Ja' and 'Nein' poles
are not dispelled even by the written word, which unites
them. In the 'Großer Dankgesang an Hans Arp' Usinger,
referring to Arp's use of paradox, speaks of:

> die schrecklichen Silben Ja und Nein,
> Gewaltiger als die Zähne der Bestie.
> Aus Ja und Nein gefügt,
> Türmen sich hinauf und hinab
> Himmel und Hölle:
> Höchste Rose des Lichts und
> Unterster Brände infernalisches Rot.(43)

Like Usinger, Arp has a conception of a universal love
which extends to the whole of creation; this 'unifies'
in that it incorporates even the most conflicting elements,
but it cannot obliterate the distinctions between them.
Nor would it be to man's advantage to do so. In another
poem, Usinger puts these words into the mouth of 'Gott',
who is addressing mankind:

> Ihr liebet das
> Unmögliche: zu sein und
> Ungetrennt. Ich habe euch
> Gegeben das Mögliche:
> Zwischen Ländern die Meere,
> Das Schwert auf das Lager
> Zwischen die Liebenden.(44)

It is not given to man to comprehend the links between
the various facets of existence – part of the human lot
is to live in a 'divided' world. In a geographical sense
this means a division of the planet earth into sea and
land, two physically very different environments which
work together to sustain human life; and in a spiritual
sense, the presence of the emotions love and hate in mankind is perhaps the most forceful proof of opposing tendencies existing side by side. Usinger's God affirms the
immense distance which separates Him from His creation:

> Ich kann mich
> Aller meiner Sterne nicht
> Erinnern, und Namen habe ich ihnen
> Nicht gegeben. Ich
> Bedarf dessen nicht.
> Vergessen will ich
> Meine Geschöpfe. Sie sollen
> Allein leben.(45)

God is no longer a loving God who cares for His creation
and wants to 'save' them, but He is a God who exists, at
least potentially, in all of creation, both good and bad.
Usinger approves the sentiments expressed in this poem by
William Blake:

> The pride of the peacock is the glory of God.
> The lust of the goat is the bounty of God.
> The wrath of the lion is the wisdom of God.
> The nakedness of woman is the work of God.
> Excess of sorrow laughs. Excess of joy weeps.(46)

Every part of creation contains a part of God. Just as
joy and sorrow, love and hate, are often scarcely dist-
inguishable, so other more tangible forms of earthly
existence are one in the eyes of God:

> Dasselbe sind
> Lamm und Löwe, der
> Sieger und der
> Besiegte, und die Heimkehrenden empfängt
> Unter der Tür der Ewigkeit
> Der all-einige Vater.
> Er aber ballte
> In seiner Hand die
> Erde aus
> Ja und Nein.(47)

How this is so man will never understand, but he has not
the power to alter the system by eliminating the opposites; nor would it help him if he could do so, for the
world as he knows it would then disintegrate - into the
'cloud of cosmic dust' referred to earlier:(48)

> es würde
> Das Feste flüchtig, der Erde
> Grund durchscheinend
> Wie Wolken, daß
> Unter Flüssen uns
> Sichtbar würden
> Sternbilder aus Himmeln
> Der Antipoden.(49)

All earthly forms are dependent on a balance of forces,
'opposites' which together form a higher synthesis.
Usinger believes that man, with his special gift of
love, can assist this natural process whereby the
Logos recreates a state of unity from elements

which have evolved separately.

Usinger considers man's alienation from God, from the fundamental unifying and creative principle, to be an inherent characteristic of his life on earth, and this alienation, together with all its resultant dualities, must continue as the basis of earthly life. According to Usinger's theory, every form of life depends upon reactions produced by various sets of 'opposites':

> Nur das mathematische Sein ist widerspruchsfrei, nicht das natürliche Sein. Es gibt kein natürliches Sein ohne Widerspruch. Anstatt 'Gott schuf die Welt' kann man auch sagen 'Gott schuf den Widerspruch'.(50)

The Logos is a creative force which is neither 'good' nor 'evil' and its continuing presence is proof that a basic world-order still exists. Like the force of gravity, it is not in itself visible to man, yet its effect can be readily observed once it comes into contact with material objects. Here too a balance of opposites is evident, in this case spirit and matter, for the material world, with all its imperfections, provides a balance for the spiritually immortal Logos and enables its presence to be felt and seen in tangible forms:

> Jedoch kommt es niemals zu einer reinen Herrschaft des Worts, denn es ist 'mit Erde vermischt' und einem steten und gewaltigen Gegengewicht der Materie ausgesetzt. Jede Ordnung ist, über Gegensätze hinweg, die Statuierung eines Zusammenhangs. So kann das Wort auch nichts anderes sein als jener Geist der Liebe, der unablässig aus dem Kosmos zu emanieren scheint.(51)

In view of the special relationship existing between the poet and the Logos, Usinger considers it possible for poets to add entire new dimensions to the range and influence of the Logos. Not only the poet, however, but the whole of mankind has a duty, in Usinger's view, to fulfil the possibilities of earthly existence by developing the positive elements already present in the world.

He believes that under the aegis of love, earthly existence could be guided on the road towards perfection.

NOTES

1. Letter 25 (10.12.71).
2. Usinger, Tellurium, Neuwied, 1966, p.155.
3. Usinger, Der ewige Kampf, p.27.
4. Usinger, Tellurium, p.154.
5. Usinger, Sonette, p.12.
6. Letter 64 (10.5.73).
7. Usinger, 'Das Dichterbildnis: Das Wort und die Geheimnisse', Welt und Wort, Literarische Monatsschrift,
   4 (1948), Bad Wörishofen, p.4.
8. Usinger, Das Wort, Darmstadt, 1931, p.1.
9. Usinger, Das Wort, p.2.
10. Usinger, Das Wort, p.3.
11. Usinger, Das Wort, p.4.
12. Interview, May 1974.
13. Interview, May 1974.
14. Usinger, Das Wort, p.4.
15. Usinger, Canopus, Wiesbaden, 1968, p.52.
16. Usinger, Gedanken, Wuppertal, 1958, unpaginated.
17. Usinger, Canopus, p.52.
18. Usinger, Welt und Wort, p.5.
19. Usinger, Das Wort, p.5.
20. Usinger, Das Wort, p.6.
21. Usinger, Das Wort, p.6.
22. Letter 25 (10.12.71).
23. Usinger, Merkbücher, p.63.
24. Usinger, Das Wort, p.58.
25. Usinger, Das Wort, p.6.
26. Usinger, Notizbuch, Darmstadt, 1966, p.30.
27. For example, in the essay 'Ja und Nein der Zeit',
    Gesichter und Gesichte, pp.91-95.
28. 'The doctrine of the Two Contraries seems to make a
    peculiar appeal to some deep-seated instinct in the
    human mind', J. Read, Prelude to Chemistry, London,
    1931, p.21.

29. The Encyclopaedia of Philosophy, London, 1967, Vol.III, p.478.
30. ibid.
31. Letter 19 (5.11.71).
32. Usinger, Die Geheimnisse, Darmstadt, 1937, pp.84-85.
33. Usinger, Die Geheimnisse, p.85.
34. C. R. Barker, 'Fritz Usinger: Poet, Essayist and Critic.' p.649 (notes on the sestinas enclosed with letter 58).
35. Letter 49 (24.10.72).
36. Letter 25 (10.12.71).
37. Usinger, Das Wort, p.4.
38. Usinger, Canopus, p.52.
39. Usinger, Die Geheimnisse, p.16.
40. Usinger, Der Stern Vergeblichkeit, Munich, 1962, p.48.
41. Usinger, Der Stern Vergeblichkeit, p.59.
42. Usinger, Die Geheimnisse, p.8.
43. Usinger, Canopus, p.23.
44. Usinger, Die Geheimnisse, p.97.
45. Usinger, Die Geheimnisse, p.97.
46. The Prophetic Writings of William Blake, Oxford, 1957, Vol.I, pp.15-16.
47. Usinger, Die Stimmen, Darmstadt, 1934, p.93.
48. Usinger, see above, p.32.
49. Usinger, Die Stimmen, p.94.
50. Usinger, Notizbuch, p.45.
51. Usinger, Welt und Wort, p.5.

CHAPTER 3

THE POET AS ALCHEMIST

Alchemy is too readily regarded as no more than a practice
developed by medieval cranks in order to extract money
from the gullible who believed that lead could be transformed into gold. That this view is an over-simplification
has been underlined by John Read:

> Alchemy, often narrowly defined as the pretended
> art of transmuting base metals into silver and
> gold, was in reality a grandiose system of phil-
> osophy, embodying a field of human beliefs and
> ideas vast in range and extending in time over
> a period of more than a thousand years.(1)

Not only is alchemy the precursor of modern chemistry,
since many alchemists (including its less honest pract-
itioners) possessed an intimate knowledge of experimental
science: it is moreover a complex philosophical system
which relates closely to Eastern religions and medieval
mysticism. The true alchemists were concerned with the
search for truth and perfection in all spheres. The
supposed properties of the Philosophers' Stone were not
confined to the transmutation of other metals into gold,
but extended to the realm of medicine, particularly as an
agent of rejuvenation, and in allegorical terms the alchemist's quest can be likened to man's pursuit of the
ideal:

> In its fullest aspect, the quest was dominated
> by a singularly noble ideal, for it was imperfect
> man's search after perfection.(2)

It is this facet of alchemy, the aspiration to present
the world with a means of achieving perfection, which
most interests Usinger and leads him to compare the roles
of poet and alchemist.
     The first evidence of an interest in alchemy on
Usinger's part is a series of five poems under the heading

'Tabula Smaragdina' in the collection Die Geheimnisse, published in 1937. The Emerald Table is the name given to the thirteen precepts upon which medieval alchemy is based, supposedly written down by Hermes Trismegistos, who himself forms the subject of an essay by Usinger in Medusa (1940). Alchemy has proved a lifelong interest for Usinger, and his latest collection of essays, Die Verwandlungen (1971), which is subtitled 'Zur Alchimie der Welt', is devoted to this theme and contains the life-histories of several alchemists.

A definition which Usinger gives of the function of poet and artist closely resembles the above statement regarding the alchemist's 'search after perfection': 'Dichter und Künstler haben uns immer wieder gezeigt, wie man die Welt vollenden könnte.'(3) The alchemist controls and perfects matter and the poet does the same with words: both activities have an element of mystery and both are enduring. Although the alchemists believed that the Philosophers' Stone, their equivalent of the poet's words, had the power to transform other materials and render them perfect, Usinger does not attribute the same value to the words of a poem, but regards their power as strictly limited. He expresses this figuratively in the sonnet 'Genius des Worts':

> Dir wird die Erde nie zum heißen Tiegel,
> Drin umzuschmelzen allen Stoffs Gestalt.
> Denn dein Geheimnis ist das Bild im Spiegel.(4)

Words cannot recreate matter, they cannot 'melt down' existing forms as the alchemists melted down metals and reconstruct them according to the wishes of the poet or philosopher. Words can only record what is there, or more precisely what appears to be there, for man lives 'am farbigen Abglanz'.

Despite these limitations, however, Usinger invests poetry with the same divinity which the alchemists attributed to their work, and he often refers to the 'holy writings' of poets:

> Lies in Büchern, was die Dichter stiften,
> Lies dein Leben lang die heiligen Schriften.(5)

Usinger frequently employs the term 'gold' as an indication
of the enduring value which he associates with the written
word:

> Die höchsten Worte trübt der Erde Rauch.
> Aus heiligen Büchern nimm der Silben Gold.(6)

Usinger often refers to the books and other possessions he
has collected over the years as 'das Gold der Jahrhunderte'
(7) or 'das Gold der Zeit'(8), and in the following quotation he applies the epithet 'golden' to his collection of
alchemical works:

> Die goldenen Büchertitel verraten dir
> Die alten Geheimnis-Wisser,
> Nostradamus und der Magier größten,
> Eliphas Levi, der das höchste Geheimnis
> Erfuhr von Hermes Trismegistos.(9)

The phrase 'golden book-titles' has, of course, a figurative
as well as a literal meaning. It was noted above that for
the alchemists too the 'gold' which they sought was, as the
most perfect metal, symbolic of other 'higher' values. In
a recent letter, Usinger comments on this aspect of alchemy:

> Die Alchimie (ist) bemüht, die verschiedenen Stoffe
> der Materie gleichzeitig als geistige Rangstufen anzu-
> sehen, an deren Spitze als höchste Rangstufe das Gold
> steht, nicht wegen seiner äußerlichen Kostbarkeit,
> sondern weil es die göttlichste Materie-Stufe ist.(10)

Gold, then, was important to the alchemist not only because
of its worth in monetary terms, but also as a symbol of
a corresponding spiritual value.

This approach of the spiritual realm via the material
is parallelled by Usinger's own attitude. He is fascinated
by the innumerable forms which occur in the constituent
material of the universe and subscribes to the alchemical
view that 'materia' is a living substance with inherent
divine properties. His poem 'Materia' indicates the

multiple forms adopted by matter and their relationship
with the spiritual realm:

> Dunkles Wesen, wie wir dich auch nennen:
> Vater, Mutter, Sohn und Geist,
> Unerschöpflich im Bekennen,
> Aber nie verratend, wer du seist:
>
> Feurig brichst du aus den Höllengründen,
> Fällst als Flocke aetherher und leicht.
> Und wir sinnen, dich zu künden,
> Einzigen Eines, das sich niemals gleicht.(11)

Like the alchemists, Usinger takes the view that matter,
being created by God, is itself divine and eternal. He
regards alchemy as a counter to Christianity and other
religions which divide the world into an 'upper' and a
'lower' region, with God, spirit and goodness occupying
the upper region and mankind, matter and evil the lower.
For the alchemist, there is no incommensurate distance
between the two spheres, for there is no absolute distinction between spirit and matter. Usinger too considers
these simply as two manifestations of one creative
principle.

> Das Schöpfungsgeheimnis ... offenbart sich uns als
> etwas Unfaßbares, zu dessen Natur es zu gehören
> scheint, daß es keinen Unterschied zwischen Sicht-
> barem und Unsichtbarem macht. Es bewegt sich auf
> beiden Ebenen, als ob es nur eine wäre mit belang-
> losen Übergängen.(12)

The fundamental principle of alchemy is the unity of all
things. This notion, like many of the basic ideas of
alchemy, developed among the Greek philosophers. Heraclitus, for example, declared that fire was the prima
materia, the principle of all things, the concrete
manifestation of the Logos. Heraclitus regarded gener-
ation as an ascending road and decomposition as a de-
scending road, but insisted that the two roads were
fundamentally part of the same process, an 'ever-living
fire, kindling in measures and being extinguished in

measures'.(13) Usinger's admiration for Heraclitus has
already been mentioned, and it is to him that he attributes
the fundamental principle of all alchemy:

> ... Heraklit, der wußte
> Der Geheimnisse größtes,
> Daß der Weg
> Nach oben derselbe sei
> Wie der nach unten:
> Goldener Satz der Alchemie.(14)

'What is below is like that which is above, and what is
above is like that which is below'(15) is the most important of the three precepts written down by Hermes
Trismegistos, since it crystallises the basic principle
of unity. Usinger points out that this precept originated
not from Hermes, but from Heraclitus, and its correspondence with his law of strife and polarity is evident.

The sentence 'Der Weg nach oben und nach unten ist ein
und derselbe' recurs constantly throughout Usinger's work
and could be described as a guiding principle of his philosophy. In the essay 'Schicksal der europäischen Kultur'
in Gesichter und Gesichte (1965), Usinger describes these
words of Heraclitus as a prophetic statement standing at
the beginning of the cultural development of Europe:

> Das besagt, daß die Welt ein einheitliches Ganzes
> ist, nicht hierarchisch gestuft in eine himmlische,
> bessere und eine irdische, schlechtere Hälfte, sondern
> überall gefügt aus denselben Elementen. Wohin man
> auch vorschreitet, die Begegnung mit der Welt ist
> immer die gleiche. Heraklit trifft hier eine qualit-
> ative Bestimmung der Welt, die später mit ganz ander-
> en Mitteln von Kopernikus, Kepler und Giordano Bruno
> wieder aufgenommen wird.(16)

Scientific investigations have established that all sub-
stances are unified in a physical sense by the fact that
they are all composed of atoms, and space-probes, together
with astrological observations, have substantiated the
view that the world is not, in physical terms at least,

divided into an upper and lower region. In philosophical
terms, the Logos serves as the unifying factor, for it
exists throughout the whole universe, both 'oben' and
'unten', and renders impossible any absolute division
between the material world and the world of higher reality:

> Das Wichtige ... ist, daß beide Welthälften, Oben
> und Unten, Geist und Materie, Licht und Dunkel,
> Gold und Blei, nicht etwas ursprünglich und wesen-
> haft anderes seien.(17)

It is evident that the alchemists do not seek to abolish
all distinctions: indeed, it is on the distinction between
gold and lead that their prospective wealth and fame rests.
Like Usinger, the alchemists adopt the notion of the Two
Contraries as the ruling forces operating in the universe
and are aware that the differences between the two poles
are as essential as the fact that they originate from
the same source. They too consider the unity of the world
to be a balance of opposites which results in a third,
unified state.

In 'Porta liborum', a poem from the 'Tabula Smaragdina'
series, Usinger speaks of finding 'das zeitenübersteigende
Wort, das bindet dir alles'.(18) This poem contains much
alchemical imagery, and reference is made to the snake
and the scorpion, both of which are portrayed frequently
in the works of the alchemists. For Usinger, both creatures represent the forces of evil and destruction - but
only in terms of earthly existence, for in eternity they
too will have their place in a fully integrated totality.
The alchemists were already able to regard the serpent
and scorpion in this way, for they had found 'das zeitenübersteigende Wort', the symbol of unity which renders
such creatures harmless. Usinger comments:

> Aus solchem
> Geheimnis sind die
> Bücher gemacht.(19)

The alchemists often depicted this unity as the union of

the Sun-god and Moon-goddess, the male and female principles
from which a child is born, usually synonymous with the
Stone. (This process was sometimes depicted as male and
female serpents devouring each other). In the poem 'Die
Waage' in Die Geheimnisse, Usinger employs the image of
a pair of scales, another important part of the alchemist's
equipment. He envisages light shining from the scales
when both sides are equally weighted:

> Und es meint dies stille Zeichen,
> Daß die Wahrheit solche Zwei
> Und die Drei ganz ohnegleichen
> Und vollkommne Schönheit sei.(20)

This unity does not simply exist as an idea, as a hypo-
thesis in the mind of poet or alchemist, but is to be
found in Nature, which is a living force filled with possibilities. In Das Glück (1947) Usinger writes:

> ... klage nicht um Verlorenes! Nimm meine Hand und
> Komm! Der Magier spricht: 'Alles ist überall'.(21)

and in Die Geheimnisse:

> Erste und Letzte
> Sind gegenwärtig immer und sind
> Dasselbe. Lege die
> Hand wohin du willst, das
> Ist es.(22)

The difficulties reside in man's interpretation of reality,
which tends to operate on a purely logical basis. Usinger,
we have seen, does not consider this to be sufficient.
One means of transcending the bounds of logic is symbolism,
for it is founded upon intuition and imagination.

The alchemists gave expression to the universal truths
which they believed they had discovered in a pictorial
language which could be compared to the poet's use of
symbols. There are two main reasons for the alchemist's
widespread use of picture-language; first, symbols were
employed by primitive peoples to convey abstract ideas
long before an adequate spoken or written language was

developed, thereby acquiring an aura of tradition; secondly,
the alchemists thought their secrets too precious to be expressed in any other form than symbols which acted as a
deterrent to the 'unworthy' and could be understood only
by the adept. Many fraudulent alchemists concealed their
ignorance behind the air of mystery endowed by symbols
and even the 'genuine' alchemists encouraged obscurities
which appeared to enhance the merits of the ultimate goal.
While Usinger does not suggest that the poet should indulge
in deliberate obscurities of this kind, he sympathises with
the view that there are some fields of knowledge which surpass the bounds of human logic and cannot be expressed in
readily comprehensible terms but allow only of symbolic
interpretation. He writes in Die Geheimnisse:

> Es sind
> Deutlich die Zeichen und dunkel. Es
> Findet immer, wer
> Finden soll.(23)

The paradoxical structure of these lines is again a feature
common in alchemical writings; the Philosophers' Stone
was often introduced in the form of a riddle or antithetical statement. In the poem 'Ich schreibe den ganzen Satz',
Usinger explicitly relates the paradoxical word play to
the philosophy of unity:

> Der Sager braucht das Gesagte
> Und das Gesagte den Sager.
> ...
> Und darum schreibe ich den ganzen Satz,
> Darin Raum ist
> Für die beiden Häupter der Welt.(24)

The paradox, based on the doctrine of polarity and the re-
conciliation of opposites, indicates a fundamental unity
in life which can only be perceived by an intuitive response to forces and powers which surpass man's logic.
    Similarly, the transition between symbol and under-
standing is achieved primarily not by man's faculties
of reason but by his intuition. Symbolism helps to make

the final transition between the world of concrete reality
and the abstract world, for, while a symbol is often based
on something tangible, it has an intangible reality of its
own:

> Der Geist setzt an die Stelle des Dings gerne den
> Begriff. Der Dichter setzt mit dem Symbol an die
> Stelle des Begriffs wieder das Ding und dessen ganze
> Tiefe und Vieldeutigkeit.(25)

The symbol for Usinger has the value of a 'magic formula'
which, like the alchemists' pictorial language, is the sole
means of conveying the 'higher truths' which the poet's
words can reveal.

The symbol, or name, has the ability to conjure up
'supernatural' phenomena:

> es bleibet der
> Name alles, zu benennen von fern das
> Unbenennbare.(26)

In order to achieve this result, however, it is necessary
to find the right magic formula, and this may take many
years:

> Bereitet aber
> Muß ein Name werden jahrlang, dann
> Saget er alles.
> Schwer ist zu finden das Wort, und es
> Suchet oft ein
> Jahrhundert vergebens.
> Doch, der es hat, verschenken
> Kann er es nicht.(27)

The long period of preparation required may be compared to
the alchemists' lifelong search for the Philosophers'
Stone, particularly since Usinger frequently refers to
this long-prepared and unique formula as 'gold':

> die Zeit
> Macht ihm sein Gold nur tiefer reif und schön.(28)

Once the appropriate symbol has been found, it retains its

value, and by 'naming' an intangible force gives the poet
a certain power over it. The passing of time only serves
to strengthen the symbol, and even fire cannot destroy it:

> Lege das Gold in das Feuer! Es wird dauern.(29)

The importance of fire in the world of the alchemist is
fundamental, since it is the chief agent in the process of
transmutation. Many properties were attributed to fire,
but most important was its supposed power over life and
death. Fire 'kills' the individual properties of the
metals, and then through its creative force a new and purer
form is created.

The doctrine of transmutation has much in common with
the mystical doctrine of the regeneration of man. Just as
the base metals must be stripped of those features which
distinguished them from the prima materia, so man, according
to the mystics, must shed his individuality and his worldly
passions in order to achieve unity with the objective reality of God. It was noted earlier that Usinger's interest
in mysticism is chiefly concerned with the mystic's attitude
to death, 'dying' in order to be born again, and much of
the imagery he employs in his poetry belongs to a complex
of imagery shared by alchemists and mystics.(30) The poem
'Das große Werk' in Die Geheimnisse is an example of Usinger's use of such imagery:

> Das Leben hat den Tod zur Speise.
> Das Helle nährt sich aus der Nacht.
> Es braucht der Feind des Feindes Weise,
> Denn anders wird es nicht vollbracht.
>
> Dann ist ein Odem und ein Hauchen.
> Der Qualm verflattert, Asche fliegt.
> Es bläst ein Mund aus toten Rauchen
> Die Flamme, die sich webt und wiegt.(31)

The notion of life feeding on death and thus forming part
of the eternal cycle of existence is common to both
alchemy and mysticism. Nature as a whole can be said
to live by virtue of these opposites in the same way that
man lives by rhythmical pulsation and inhalation. The

plant furnishes a clear example of a 'death', or return
to primal matter, for it returns to the earth from which
it came and from which, in most cases, it will grow again.
The alchemist seeks to imitate this process by reducing
metals to a fluid state, hoping thereby to generate a new,
more 'perfect' substance.

Although Usinger rejects the notion of a primal element,
he accords to fire a principle role in the origins and end
of all material life:

> Es gibt keinen Urstoff, sondern nur Welt. Die für unser
> Begreifen anfängliche Weltstufe ist die feurige.
> Auch die Welt im großen besteht aus Alchimie, nur
> daß das Feuer aus seinen Flammen selbst den Stern
> der Weisen hervorbringt.(32)

Usinger regards the contemporary theory that the origin of
planetary systems is due to the condensation of hot masses
of gas produced by the sun as a modern equivalent of the
theory proposed by Heraclitus. A release of atomic energy
of sufficient magnitude, it is believed, reduces the planets to flame once more.(33)

In a poem entitled 'Die Elemente', Usinger follows the
alchemists in making fire the chief agent in the life-
cycle:

> Anfang und Ende ist hier all-zugleich.
> Die Glut gebiert den Stoff, die Glut verschlingt
> Den Stoff zu guter Letzt.
> Das Feuer bleibt:
> Die Reinheit Feuer und die Lohe Tod.(34)

Fire is endowed with the ability not only to destroy and
create, but also to purify. For Usinger, as a poet,
purification is even more closely associated with the
creation of form than it was for the alchemists. He
refers to himself as a salamander, able to live in the
fire and give it coherent meaning:

> Ich verschenke
> Die Form den Flammen.(35)

Fire is here identified with the chaos which preceded the
creation of the world. The apparent formlessness which
fire represents is converted into visible form by the
poet:

> Ich Gestalt und Ungestalt
> In dem Feuer, das mich nährt:
> Eines ist, das dröhnt und hallt
> Und das ewig währt.(36)

The poet himself is an individual form, yet becomes formless in that his consciousness merges with the world in its
constant state of flux and change. Out of this state of
chaos he again creates individual forms through his poetry.
The salamander-poet, in a state of creativity, sees and
hears the outside world through the transforming and unifying haze of the fire by which he is surrounded. Usinger
often refers to the 'fire' of his words. What appears to
be chaos in fact contains the seeds of the purest forms;
fire represents a kingdom behind all forms, a kingdom in
which the poet dwells.

The poet also purifies and regenerates through his
transformation of diverse subjects into poetry. Like fire
and the alchemist, he transforms the temporal into the
eternal by reducing the object of his poem to its basic
and immortal elements. This procedure is described in
'Der Schöpfer':

> In kleinem Kreis Welt zu Welten schaffend,
> Das Fernste lade ich zu meiner Schwelle,
> Und Flüchtiges im Fluge noch erraffend,
> Zieh ich das Dunkle zu mir her ins Helle.
>
> Versammelt sei um mich der Hermen Reihe.
> Dem Sinne ist Geringstes nicht gering.
> Und willst du, Wort, daß ich dir Leben leihe,
> So tritt aus meinem Haupt und werde Ding!(37)

The words 'der Hermen Reihe' refer to the numerous alchemical works of the 'sons of Hermes' which Usinger
possesses. Although both poet and alchemist appear to
work within a very limited sphere, they are concerned with

the fundamental meaning of existence, with Nature as a
living and unified force and with its relationship to man;
this gives their work a significance beyond its immediate
value.

Hence, the parallels which Usinger finds between poet
and alchemist are not confined to his interpretation of
their common mission as a search for eternal truths, but
extend also to the methods they both employ in this quest.
Man is encouraged to seek spiritual perfection not outside
the earthly sphere, but in the sublimation of some of the
fundamental principles of the natural world. Usinger vis-
ualises the poet or alchemist as an agent who endeavours
to select and cultivate those natural principles which
are likely to lead towards an ideal state and to elimin-
ate those which threaten chaos and destruction. Usinger
makes the following comment on the alchemist's selective
approach to the natural world:

> Während ... die Natur gleichzeitig aufwärts und
> abwärts wirkt, versucht die Alchimie, die empordring-
> enden Tendenzen der Natur zu beförden: die Bildung
> des Edleren, Heilsamen, Zusammenhaltenden. Eine
> welt-therapeutische Tendenz ist ihr eigen. Die Welt
> soll aus den ihr zugehörigen Kräften heraus geheilt
> werden.(38)

The alchemist focusses his attentions towards form and
perfection and not in the opposite direction, although
it is equally present in Nature. Similarly, while the
prevailing tendency among contemporary poets and writers
is towards the destructive and the negative, Usinger remains true to the traditional modes, exploring relationships between existing forms and seeking to produce new
and enduring forms of his own.

Poetry and its symbolism is, of course, only one kind
of transformation which the Logos, or living force of
Nature, undergoes. Nature's creative powers are seen in
flowers, trees and animals as well as in man himself, and
the changes which take place in all these things are part
of Nature's alchemy: for example, winter turns into

spring, flowers bloom and die, vegetation can produce coal and even diamonds. Usinger believes, however, that the imagination can act as a supplementary force, providing what Nature cannot. Man alone possesses imagination, and he can use this to interpret the laws of nature in ways unique to him. Thus each artist, writer or musician transforms an idea, emotion or object into the form appropriate to him; each of these forms then has the value of a natural object and should be regarded in the same way as these - as a 'living symbol'.

Thus, while it is no longer amongst men's most pressing concerns to melt down lead in the hope of making gold, the beliefs which prompted this endeavour have not lost their validity but have their parallel in the work of a poet like Usinger who shares their faith in the ultimate unity of all creation. Although the visible rift between spirit and matter has gradually increased, the imagination is capable of restoring an image of unity since it can make transitions which defy logic, regarding spirit and matter as part of the natural polarity which maintains all life. Usinger commends the alchemist's unprejudiced treatment of all spheres of life as one whole, as one Nature, infused with the same animating spirit of the Logos, since this corresponds to his own view that the creations of man's mind, providing that these are in harmony with natural laws, form part of the basic life-force. Usinger, as we shall see, believes that even the formless regions of the cosmos may be expressed in symbolical terms which are meaningful to man's imagination if not to his logical capacities.

NOTES

1. J. Read, The Alchemist in Life, Literature and Art, London, 1947, p.1.
2. J. Read, Prelude to Chemistry, London, 1931, p.118.
3. Usinger, Die Verwandlungen, Mainz, 1971, p.71.
4. Usinger, Die Stimmen, p.15.

5. Usinger, Der Stern Vergeblichkeit, p.11.
6. Usinger, Das Glück, Darmstadt, 1947, p.23.
7. Usinger, Canopus, p.50.
8. Usinger, Der Planet, Darmstadt, 1972, p.57.
9. Usinger, Der Planet, p.57.
10. Letter (10.10.75).
11. Usinger, Die Geheimnisse, p.26.
12. Usinger, Merkbücher, pp.7-8.
13. Encyclopaedia Britannica, 14th ed., Vol. II, p.386.
14. Usinger, Der Planet, p.76.
15. Translation taken from J. Read, Prelude to Chemistry, p.54.
16. Usinger, Gesichter und Gesichte, p.8.
17. Usinger, Medusa, Dessau, 1940, p.76.
18. Usinger, Die Geheimnisse, p.112.
19. Usinger, Die Geheimnisse, p.19.
20. Usinger, Die Geheimnisse, p.19.
21. Usinger, Das Glück, p.40.
22. Usinger, Die Geheimnisse, pp.104-5.
23. Usinger, Die Geheimnisse, p.104.
24. Usinger, Canopus, p.18.
25. Usinger, Merkbücher, p.14.
26. Usinger, Die Geheimnisse, p.109.
27. Usinger, Die Geheimnisse, p.109.
28. Usinger, Hermes, Darmstadt, 1942, p.90.
29. Usinger, Der Stern Vergeblichkeit, p.36.
30. Of the many mystics who show an interest in alchemy, the most important is the seventeenth-century mystic, Jakob Boehme, who made considerable use of alchemical language in his writings. In his book Goethe, The Alchemist, Cambridge, 1952, Ronald Gray includes a chapter entitled 'Jakob Boehme and Alchemy', in which he draws numerous parallels between Boehme's thought and that of the alchemist. Gray describes Boehme as 'the man who imposed a pattern on the alchemical symbols and thus introduced them into the stream of current thought'.(p.37) Usinger is well acquainted with the works of Boehme.
31. Usinger, Die Geheimnisse, p.14.
32. Usinger, Merkbücher, p.17.

33. Usinger expresses this theory in poetic form in 'Ignus universalis', from his latest collection of poems <u>Die himmlische Heimkehr</u>, which at the time of writing is still in manuscript form:

> Mutter du der Welten, Feuer,
> Alles quillt aus deinem Schoße,
> Das an Herrlichkeiten Große
> Und das Ungeheuer.
>
> Wie du solche Welten schaffest,
> Daß sie allwärts funkelnd schweifen,
> Keiner wird es je begreifen,
> Da du andre raffest
>
> Heimwärts in die Feuerschöße,
> Wo sie werden, was sie waren,
> Doch erhebst den wunderbaren
> Stern der höchsten Größe.

34. Usinger, <u>Canopus</u>, p.34.
35. Usinger, <u>Canopus</u>, p.34.
36. Usinger, <u>Die Geheimnisse</u>, p.43.
37. Usinger, <u>Die Geheimnisse</u>, p.12.
38. Usinger, <u>Die Verwandlungen</u>, p.9.

CHAPTER 4

MYTHOLOGY

For the Greeks of the Homeric period and for most subsequent writers, the terms logos and mythos represent
two antithetical modes of thought. Logos denotes objective truth or reason which, as a law of Nature, does
not itself have intelligence or consciousness yet lends
order and regularity to the movement of things. Mythos,
on the other hand, ultimately came to denote that which
cannot really exist, a product of the imagination having
nothing in common with man's powers of reason or with
the ordered system of laws governing the universe.
Usinger, we have seen, regards reason and imagination
not as antithetical but as complementary: not only is
the imagination capable of going beyond the bounds of
logic; inversely, reason can be brought to bear on in-
ventions of the imagination. Although mythology is
devised by man's imaginative faculties, it is designed
to fulfil as vital a function as any rationally conceived
system, namely, to answer questions appertaining to the
nature and purpose of the universe and man's position in
it. Just as Usinger avoids equating the Logos with human
logic, he views mythology as more than a mere series of
legends of man's own devising. Like the Logos, mythological figures have an independent existence in Usinger's
view, or rather they represent forces which exist outside
man.

Far from experiencing any conflict between the concepts
logos and mythos, Usinger describes the Logos itself as a
myth:

Auch das Wort Logos ist ein Mythos. Es bezeichnet
ein Sein, dem wir verschiedene Qualitäten zusprechen,
ohne daraus nun eine bestimmte Gestalt zu formen.
Das Mythologische spielt in meiner Dichtung deshalb
eine so große Rolle, weil sie häufig von außer- und
übermenschlichen Kräften handelt, für die uns genauere
Bestimmungen fehlen, so daß wir uns immer wieder in

die Bereiche mythischer Namen flüchten müssen.(1)

Where empirical knowledge is inadequate and logic's precise definitions are unable to describe phenomena which occur, namely, in matters concerning the mysterious spiritual life of the universe, Usinger employs mythological concepts.

Although it is the Logos which is the principle of order underlying all creation, Usinger seeks to bring some kind of identity to the remoter parts of the cosmos through a hierarchy of mythological creatures. They are representative of a spiritual dimension beyond man's understanding, whose physical representative is Nature. In this Usinger differs from Hölderlin, for whom there were only 'Götter' and 'Menschen', the gods being inseparable from Nature. Usinger's mythology is eclectic, being primarily a combination of the doctrines of Heraclitus and the Homeric myths of Ancient Greece, but also incorporating elements of mysticism and basic Christianity. As well as the gods and heroes of the Homeric legends, angels, saints, and Jesus Christ all play a symbolic role in Usinger's thought.

While he considers the Christian solution to the problems of existence to be as unsatisfactory as that of the Greeks for the modern world, Usinger feels it necessary to come to terms with Christianity, particularly with the figure of Christ Himself, whose influence has been greater and more enduring than that of any other historical figure. Usinger proposes the same solution as Hölderlin; Christianity is transferred to the realm of myth and Christ to the ranks of the Greek gods. In a collection of essays Usinger comments:

> Der letzte der Götter war Christus. Auch er, ein
> Bruder des Herakles und des Dionysos, hat die
> Weltherrschaft schon niedergelegt.(2)

Although Christ is thus 'demoted' and denied any unique authority, the Christian God fulfils a totally different function:

Gott ist die hinter allem stehende <u>unsichtbare</u>
Gesamtmacht; die Götter sind das, was von ihm
im Natur- und Menschenbereich sichtbar und spürbar
wird!(3)

God is the creative force behind all things and the Logos
is equivalent to the mind of God, residing both in the
individual and in the universe at large. The gods represent intangible and inexplicable forces which are dis-
cernable in the world in a variety of ways. Unlike God,
they are subject to the laws of the Logos, laws which
they do not understand any more than man. In a poem entitled 'Die Götter' Usinger writes:

> Stets wieder neue, wachsend aus dem Grund,
> Den keiner kennt, auch ihr nicht ... (4)

The gods are 'ewig andere, doch ewig gleiche', eternally
present in the world yet subject to change:

> Niemals sind wir unsrer Himmel sicher,
> Und die Götter wechseln wie Gezeiten:
> Scheinen sie uns näher, feierlicher,
> Sind sie auch zugleich schon im Entgleiten.(5)

They are always 'gods', and as such are immortal, yet they
are not in control of the laws which govern the world.
   While the Greek gods had daily contact with mankind
and were anthropomorphised, the gods which figure in
Usinger's poetry are remote and impersonal. They cannot
even be identified - unlike the gods in Hölderlin's work -
with specific natural forces. The gods, in Usinger's
view, are conditioned by the dominant characteristics of
the world's successive historical eras, summoned into being
by the imagination of men, yet possessing a life of their
own:

> Die menschliche Imagination besitzt eine Kraft der
> Vorstellung und der Verwirklichung, daß sie geradezu
> die Götter zur Erscheinung zwingt, in einem solchen
> Maße, daß die so aufgerufenen Götter ihrerseits dann
> wieder auf die Menschenwelt zurück zu wirken beginnen,

so als seien sie real vorhandende Mächte mit eigenen
Kräften und schöpferischen Ideen.(6)

While the Greeks enjoyed the security of a clearly defined
and circumscribed universe, with the gods as its ultimate
meaning, modern man is surrounded by an unresponsive void
and has no certainty that any ultimate truths exist at all.
Hence the Greek gods, despite their supposed power over
man's destiny, reflected the security of the Greeks and
inspired confidence by their general resemblance to human
beings in both appearance and behaviour. The modern view
of the universe, as Usinger stresses constantly, is utterly different, and it is difficult to envisage man's appeals
or threats having any effect on the planets and the void
of an infinite universe whose whole nature is so alien to
his own.

The remoteness of the gods is reflected in their
silence - there is no longer any communication possible
between gods and men. This is not a choice on the part
of the gods, a decision to remain aloof from all human
activities, but is determined by Fate, by the laws of the
Logos:

> Wer gab den Göttern
> Den Mund,
> Daß sie nun schweigen? (7)

The silence of the cosmos is a modern phenomenon: the
Greek gods conversed with man, but there is no longer any
possibility of attaining the same level of contact. Living in the twentieth century, Usinger conceives of divine
beings which are defined by a peaceful and unconscious
participation in creation, irrespective of man's wishes.
The poet fulfils a similar function in relation to the
gods as with the Logos: he gives expression to the silent
presence of the gods and the ways in which this presence
affects the life of man. Paradoxically, the gods in their
eternity need the existence of a time-bound world in order
to manifest themselves:

Die Götter
Bedürfen, daß sie erscheinen, der
Vergangenheit. (8)

The poet records the changes which take place in the
manifestations assumed by the gods and thereby gives
meaning to their existence, for, like the God of Usinger's
early poems, the gods live in a permanently fulfilled
moment with no sense of temporal perspective or of their
own position in the world.

Like the God of the mystics, then, Usinger's gods
need mankind, and specifically the poet. Thus it is
that, although they do not communicate directly with
man, they are a source of inspiration to him. In 'Die
Götter lesen nicht', Usinger asserts that 'die Götter
leuchten' (9), which is an acknowledgement of the
inspiration they give. They represent ideas which are
of great value to modern man, who is growing further
away from spiritual values in an age of materialism:

> So bleiben, da des Lebens wir arm geworden sind,
> Götter und Göttinnen nur, Mythengestalten,
> Die uns sagen: so solltet ihr sein,
> Um überhaupt zu sein, um als
> Wesen zu zählen. (10)

It could be argued that 'gods' are more important to the
world of the twentieth century than they were to the
Ancient Greeks, who valued spiritual principles as a
matter of course.

One such principle, which Usinger feels is becoming
ever more remote from the human sphere, is represented
by Aphrodite, the goddess of love and beauty. In an
early poem, 'Aphrodite anadyomen', Usinger appeals to
the goddess to appear once more and restore beauty to
the world, and in a later poem he declares that he often
feels her presence, the presence of beauty as an idea,
to be more readily accessible than any human manifestations of beauty:

Warum, o Göttin, nahtest du öfter mir
    Als Menschen taten, da doch viel eher sonst
    Ein irdisch Wesen naht dem andern,
        Menschliche Grüße und Rede tauschend? (11)

Aphrodite represents an inexhaustible source of beauty, but
her beauty is abstract and needs interpretation in the
world of man.

After years of searching, Usinger finally finds a mythological symbol of his own which is capable of conveying a
sense of this transcendent beauty and perfection in the
'späte Nymphen', which first appear in <u>Niemandsgesang</u>
(1959) and later in <u>Der Stern Vergeblichkeit</u> (1962).
They are associated not with the passions as were their
Greek counterparts, but with truth and purity and its
representation in Usinger's work:

        Fremder und stiller Leser,
        Hier sieh, was ich dir schenke,
        Göttlichste Gabe auf einem Blatt Papier:
        Die späten Nymphen,
        Die schönhäuptigen,
        Vollkommenen Antlitzes,
        In silbernen Augen dunkelgroße Pupillen,
        Lippenbogen von einem wohllaut der Linien,
        Der jedes Sagen besiegt
        ...
        Hier sind sie, gezeichnet für dich
        Auf einem Blatt Papier,
        Mit Worten, mit nichts als Worten.
        Vergöttlichung der Wünsche. (12)

The nymphs bridge the gulf between the divine, Nature,
and humanity, for - unlike the gods - they have a certain
'materiality'; they represent the essence of Nature's
perfections, and their physical appearance is as important as the spiritual values for which they stand.
It is the 'späte Nymphen' which prompt Hagen to speak
of Usinger's creation of his own mythology,(13) for
Usinger's nymphs are not only completely transformed in
both appearance and symbolical import, they have assumed

a far greater significance than the minor rustic deities
of Greek mythology. Equally important, the nymphs are a
readily communicable symbol - not a private expression,
but one which can lay claim to universality.

In complete antithesis to the nymphs stands the symbol
of Medusa in Usinger's work, representing all that is
'unnatural'. Usinger identifies beauty with inner perfection - not beauty as the embodiment of moral goodness,
as was the case with Schiller, but as an expression of
inner harmony of spirit. The Greeks personified this
ideal of life in their gods. Aphrodite, the most beautiful
of their deities, is the individual representative of the
harmony which reigned throughout the Greek world. Usinger's
un-named 'späte Nymphen' similarly express the harmony
which, although no longer to be found in the world of man,
still exists in Nature. For Usinger, Medusa constitutes
the opposite extreme - ugliness depicting disharmony. It
is partly the fact that she was once beautiful which makes
her such an intriguing figure for Usinger, and she comes
to symbolise the Schein/Sein duality in life; what at
first sight appears to be beautiful can soon reveal itself
to be exactly the opposite:

> Das Schöne ist
> Furchtbar. Denn selten
> Sieht einer
> Schlangenhaar und den
> Giftigen Gürtel. (14)

Medusa represents a threat not simply to the individuals
who come into contact with her, but, by extension in
symbolic terms, to the harmony of the whole universe.
Thus she stands for the divided world - a world in which
appearances belie inner qualities. She is inimical to
all life, the complete antithesis of Nature's creative
forces:

> Urgründig Haupt, von Schlangen wild gekrönt,
> Ihr Lippen eisig, Blick, der jäh versteint:
> Wer schuf es, daß er einmal dich versöhnt,
> Und wer, daß dieses Auge einmal weint?

> Wo ist ein Letztes, Herrlichstes und rührt
> Dein totes Herz, daß sich aus seinem Grund
> Ein Glück erlöst, ein Wunder dich verführt
> Und langsam lächeln machte diesen Mund? (15)

Usinger regards the snakes which adorn Medusa's head as
the epitome of a 'negative', destructive power. (16)
In addition, one look from her turns living creatures
into stone, which again underlines her destructive nature.

Usinger's mythological figures are further indications
of his belief in a system of polarity. Even Medusa is a
servant of Fate, and so too is the traditional god of
chaos, Dionysus. Dionysus was originally an Asiatic
wine-god, but Usinger follows the Greek tradition in
taking a much broader view of him as the representative
of all the powers of chaos in contrast to Apollo, the
god of order:

> Der Gott des Alls, der alles lieh,
> Glücksrausch und Todesnot. (17)

Significantly, Dionysus is both a source of intense
pleasure and potentially fatal for man. Usinger describes Apollo in similarly ambiguous terms:

> Herr der tödlichen Pfeile, der du
> Das Geschoß
> Schickst mit der Offenbarung
> In die Kehle des Lieblings. (18)

There are any number of contradictions in Apollo's relationship with his protégé, the poet: he can grant him
a successful union with the sublime laws he represents,
or he can destroy him, just like Dionysus. The decision
does not reside with Apollo himself, but is decreed by
Fate, by the Logos, which he, like all the gods, must
obey. Apollo's revelations are 'unfaßbar', like the Logos
itself: Usinger reproaches the god with inflaming his
heart and then denying him fulfilment of his aspirations.
In his Gedanken Usinger writes: 'Der Gott der Dichtung
ist grausam wie alle Götter'. (19) He regards the gods
as 'grausam' because the standards which determine their

actions do not correspond to those of the human sphere.

It is evident that Usinger regards Apollo and Dionysus in not dissimilar terms, a fact which underlines his premise that the two are essentially one and the same: 'Im Grund sind beide dasselbe: die Totalität des Lebens, von zwei Seiten gesehen'.(20) The same life-forces are present in both gods, but in Dionysus they are in a chaotic state, while Apollo is the mythological expression of the ordering Logos.(21) In a letter, Usinger defines Dionysus as 'chaotische Lebenskraft (daher Wein, Seleni, Panther usw)' and Apollo as 'geordnete und ordnende Lebenskraft (daher auf seiner Seite die Musen und Dichter, die Lyra, das Licht usw)'(22).

If the poet, as the chosen of Apollo, enjoys a special relationship with the gods and the powers they represent, he is not alone in this position of privilege. The Greek concept of the 'hero' denotes an individual halfway between gods and men, his superhuman achievements brought him as near to the status of a god as was possible for a mortal. In the words of Michael Grant:

> The heroic outlook shook off primitive superstitions and taboos by showing that man can do amazing things by his own effort and by his own nature, indeed that he can almost rise above his own nature into strengths scarcely known or understood.(23)

The gods are created immortal: the heroes achieve immortality through their deeds. However, the activities of the hero are confined to one sphere, that of physical strength, and Usinger is often led to draw comparisons between the hero, the man of action, and the poet, the man of words. Both share the ability to put a temporary halt to time and change, however brief that moment may be, and both require the assistance of the gods if their achievements are to be in any way enduring:

> Wo verlassen von Göttern
> Ein Volk ist, sterben
> Helden und Dichter auch. (24)

Both poet and hero are exceptional in that they strive to
reach out beyond the accepted bounds of human achievement;
but in many respects they are opposite figures, in that one
is concerned with the spirit, the other with matter. Despite this, however, they can both work together; while the
hero performs great deeds, the poet observes them, but not
just passively - he also interprets and communicates:

> es tötet dem Täter
> Das Große immer das Große.
> Dem Seher nur ist die
> Dauer deutlich und
> Kündbar das immer gleiche
> Gesetz. (25)

The hero is in the midst of action, going from one
great deed to the next without relating one to another.
The poet has the 'Distanz' and the imagination necessary
to relate each deed meaningfully to the rest of human
history and thus give meaning to each individual act.

Although their 'cosmic' significance, seen objectively,
may be equal, Usinger appears to regard the poet's task
as both more difficult and more enduring:

> Mächtiger als Helden ist
> Das Wort. In Wäldern, geistigen,
> Davon nur schwer vernehmbar
> Ein Rauschen ist. (26)

Although it is 'das Wort' in which the power resides,
there is a suggestion that 'the pen is mightier than the
sword' and that by his contact with the Word, the poet too
becomes powerful. The Logos is again a 'Rauschen', a
scarcely perceptible hint of truth almost drowned by the
sounds of the world. The poet's power comes from being
able to perceive the 'geistige Wälder' which are concealed
from others. Part of being a hero is the worldly fame and
glory attached to the feats performed: the hero's deeds
are visible and tangible, as is his reward. The poet's
achievements, on the other hand, are in the realm of
'Geist', invisible to man, and go unrecognised:

Verboten ist die Krone
Dem Dichter. (27)

In some respects it is inappropriate that the poet should
be honoured, for he himself is not responsible for his insight, he is simply a vehicle for the communication of
spiritual truths.

It was noted earlier with reference to the role of
Christ in Usinger's work that he does not differentiate
between figures of Greek mythology and personalities drawn
from biblical sources. Usinger incorporates Greek and
Christian elements alike into his mythology, often blending
the two spheres in a single image. Thus it is that he regards the saints, in many respects, as a parallel to the
heroes, with the Christian God taking the place of Fate
and the gods. While the hero has but a temporary union
with the divine powers which leads to his own destruction,
the saint constitutes the ultimate example of a life and
death fulfilled in complete harmony with God. An aura of
tragedy surrounds both hero and saint, but in the case of
the saint it is the manner of death which distinguishes
him - he dies for his faith. While the hero is remembered
for his deeds, the saint is often a passive figure; and
whereas the hero's death destroys all his powers and aspirations, the saint finds in death not only personal fulfilment, but also a means to inspire others by his example.
With Usinger's image of the saints, the idea of life being
perfected in death re-emerges:

> Sie zahlten ohne Zagen ihren Preis:
> Den einen großen Tod, sei es in Mauern,
> Den Menschen fern, sei es am Kreuz mit Qualen.
> Doch unser sind die tausend kleinen Tode,
> Der Jahre Tod, der Liebe Tod, der Freunde. (28)

While the poet and the hero have only brief moments of
contact with the divine principle, whether this be the
Greek gods, the Logos, or the Christian God, the saint's
faith, which governs his whole life and is immortalised
in a martyr's death, is an enduring bond with God.

The saint is the only one who has truly come to terms

with a world of change which he sees in the light of the
divine. He has found a permanent state of equilibrium -
what Usinger calls 'eine ewige Gleiche' - which means
that he is beyond the reach of the conflicting emotions
which are the lot of all other mortals. Although still
subject to the laws of change whilst he lives on earth,
the eyes of the saint are continuously fixed on something
beyond, which allows him to remain unaffected by external
tribulations:

> Die Seligen, die eine ewige Gleiche
> Erfunden haben zwischen Tag und Nacht,
> Die Schwebe von Gefühl und Ungefühl,
> Darin die Seele ohne Schwanken wandelt. (29)

The saint accepts good and bad fortune with equanamity;
this allows his inner self, the soul, to develop single-
mindedly, thus giving the saint a 'Dauer im Wechsel'
which finds its culmination in death, since in death the
soul of the saint is freed completely from the world of
change and passes into the tranquility of eternal life.
In Usinger's view, the most important single lesson which
the saints teach is that death must be accepted as an inevitable part of life - not only the death which marks the
end of an individual's time on earth, but also the 'kleine
Tode', the end of a love-affair, the destruction of a town,
even the withering of a plant.
   Time and again Usinger returns to the notion of acceptance of adversity as the only means by which man can achieve stability and avoid being buffeted around by changes
in the world and within himself. In order to attain the
degree of acceptance which he advocates, it is necessary
for him to believe in some external unifying force or
forces. Despite his continued use of mystical imagery,
Usinger came to regard mysticism itself as inadequate
and introspective. In the essay-collection Medusa, (30)
he refers to mysticism as 'etwas Blaßes, Verträumtes,
in sich selbst Versunkenes, ein sanftes und wohltuendes
Sinnieren'. (31) The Christian God, as well as the
Greek gods, is revengeful, demonstrating anger as well

66

as love for mankind in the various adversities which befall him and for which mysticism, in Usinger's view,
offers no satisfactory explanation. While rejecting both
mysticism and Christianity as a philosophy of life,
Usinger does adopt some aspects of Christian teaching,
largely in a symbolic sense. The Christian relationship
between God and man is entirely different in nature from
that of Ancient Greece. The Greeks had gods to represent
most aspects of creation and most attitudes towards mankind, save for humility and charitable love. These latter
qualities, which Usinger holds to be the most important of
all, are the contribution of Christianity and are personified in Jesus Christ.

It was stated earlier that in Usinger's philosophy the
problem of whether or not Christ was the son of God does
not arise: the significance of Jesus Christ resides in
His own personality, not as the saviour of mankind, but
as the man who brought love into the world. Christian
love differs from the Greek _eros_ primarily in that it is
utterly unselfish, and is not confined to desire for a
particular person but extends to mankind as a whole.
Whilst the love of ordinary mortals is inevitably limited
to the sphere of their immediate family and acquaintance,
Christ's love has become a universal concept. It is for
this reason that Usinger includes Him in his mythological
system. It will be evident from the preceding chapters
that Usinger regards the poet as a messenger of the universal love which Christ represents, and it is therefore
not surprising to find Usinger drawing frequent analogies
between the poet and Christ. The humility which is essential to sustain this love serves as a further bond
between them.

Usinger constantly underlines the need for humility
and employs the notion of a humble life and rejection
by the world as an important distinction between poet and
hero. While the hero's achievements are not considered
successful unless accompanied by the recognition of his
fellow men, Usinger expresses the opinion that worldly
success can actually detract from the 'holiness' of the

message which the poet has to convey:

> Es soll, wer den Geist
> Sät,
> Ernten Verlassenheit, daß das Heilige
> Heilig bleibe. (32)

Neglect by the world seems inevitable for those who
cultivate spiritual values. Like Christ, the poet has
an invisible sceptre, for theirs is an invisible and
intangible kingdom, one devoted to the ultimate meaning
of life as symbolised by the biblical phrase 'Alpha und
Omega', which is 'der Worte Wort, das alle Fragen endet'
(33)   If God, who is Lord of all creation, with legions
of angels, can allow Himself to be mocked and slandered,
Usinger feels that the poet cannot complain of his humble
life, for what is the poet in comparison to God? (34)

St John identifies the Logos with the person of Christ,
but Usinger simply employs imagery from the life of Christ
in order to illustrate that the Logos, which is closely
allied to Christian love, (35) is rarely found in its expected form. The period in which the Logos was most visible on earth is for Usinger not that of the life of
Christ, but the days of Ancient Greece five centuries
earlier, when there was no rift apparent between the
spiritual and its manifestations on earth, whereas Christianity draws a clear line of demarcation between spirit
and matter. The humble origins of the rebirth of the
Logos in Christ become symbolic of its rebirth in the
works of poets, which often emerge in an equally incon-
spicuous way:

> Es haben die
> Könige gerufen unter
> Kronen, die
> Großen gewartet in
> Mänteln von Purpur. (36)

As Herod expected the Messiah to be a richly robed king
like himself, so it is generally assumed that anything
worthwhile will be accompanied by the appropriate measure
of pomp and circumstance; but the Word is born inconspic-

uously, 'versteckt und unscheinbar, wie im Neste des
Zaunkönigs'. (37)

In Usinger's view, the life of Christ demonstrates
that 'das Heilige' is always 'verschenkt an ungereifte
Zeiten' (38) because God's time and our own do not co-
incide. The poet too, in Usinger's interpretation of
his role, seems to be born out of his time and is mis-
understood by his fellow men; he too will always seem
out of step with earthly time because, like Christ,
the truths he has to communicate belong to the realm
of the eternal, whose laws cannot be encompassed by human
logic.

In Usinger's view, the principal attribute of Jesus
Christ is what he terms his 'Vergeblichkeit':

> Du Gott der Erlösung, der nichts erlöste,
> Du Gott der Vergeblichkeit,
> Es ist uns keiner nötiger als du,
> Uns die Vergeblichkeit zu lehren.
> Es muß die Liebe dort am meisten
> Geliebt werden, wo sie nicht ist,
> Und zeigen, daß das nirgends Vorhandene
> Dennoch vorhanden ist.
> ...
> Es sind die Meister der Vergeblichkeit
> Die stärksten Stützen der Welt. (39)

Although the love and humility which Christ represents
are, in the present world situation, very elusive qualities
and although it is intellectually inconceivable that universal love should ever exist as a reality, Usinger insists
that acting as if this illogical supposition were true is,
paradoxically, the only means by which mankind can hope to
bring about its fulfilment. Christ brought His message of
love to the world, and Usinger considers this to be sufficient proof of His divinity, no matter whose son He was.
He taught that love can save the world and this is in itself true, Usinger claims. Christ did die in vain in the
sense that the world has not been saved, but this is because few people practise the love He taught, not because

the message was invalid. Christ's 'Vergeblichkeit' is no
impediment to a belief in His message of love, but actually
serves as an encouragement, for Christ knew that His
martyrdom was in vain, yet this did not dissuade Him from
carrying it out. 'Vergeblichkeit ist keine Hinderungs-
kraft, sondern ein Anstoß - weil es vergeblich ist, muß
man umso mehr tun'.(40) In Der Stern Vergeblichkeit,
Usinger writes:

> Die Märtyrer gingen vergeblich durch die Folter.
> ...
> Ich weiß, daß alles in der Welt einander fremd ist.
> Dies ist kein Grund gegen das Leben.
> ...
> Lebe, als ob die Welt wahr wäre!
> Lebe, als ob die Liebe wahr wäre! (41)

As well as the figures of Christ and the saints, Usinger
includes Christian angels in his hierarchy of divine or
semi-divine creatures. Usinger's angels, like his gods,
represent remote and impersonal powers which affect the
lives of men. Usinger describes death as such an angel,
as something which does not exist in a physical form but
which is a force able to exert an influence on earthly life.
Yet these impersonal, unapproachable powers also have their
positive side. 'Der Stürzende' in Die Geheimnisse describes
the angels as 'dunkel-groß' but also as 'Trostgewalten':

> Da du dich hinweggewendet,
> Stürmen Geister, mich zu halten,
> Engel, schnelle, hergesendet,
> Dunkel-große Trostgewälten.(42)

Usinger's angels differ from his concept of the gods in
that they help man by preventing him from being overwhelmed by an unbearable burden of suffering. Seelbach
describes them as 'helfende Trostgewalten der ewigen
Liebe'.(43)
   The above stanza implies that the angels - unlike the
gods - are sent expressly to man and not to the rest of
creation. The remaining stanzas from 'Der Stürzende'

support this view; there is a 'Geist der Tränen', a
'Geist der Treue', a 'Geist der letzten Einsamkeiten', a
'Geist der abgestorbenen Zeiten', and there are 'Geister
der Erinnerungen', 'Geister der lebendigen Toten', 'Geister
aller Traumeszungen'. The most important of these spirits
and the only one to be described as an 'Engel' is the last
named 'Engel der Vergessenheit':

> Und mein Haupt, sich ganz vertrauend,
> Sinkt an eine Schulter breit.
> Ich erkenn dich, aufwärts schauend,
> Engel der Vergessenheit. (44)

This angel is, in a sense, the link between man and the
incomprehensible forces which control him or which pursue
their course regardless of him, for the 'Engel der Vergessenheit' provides a two-fold 'safety-valve': first, it allows
man to forget much that would otherwise make life unbearable,
and secondly, it denies him complete knowledge:

> Solches
> Schutzgeistes bedürfen wir, daß
> Nicht der Gedanke uns die
> Schläfen zertrümmre. (45)

Man is granted knowledge of many things, but one thought
is kept from him, for it is 'das Entsetzliche'. The angel
is able to remain unaffected by what it knows, but is careful to shield mankind from it. Usinger describes the angel
as the 'ältester Geist der Welt': it was there before all
time and witnessed the birth of everything in the world;
it is dedicated to preserving life, 'ein Geist des Lebens';
and gives man the courage he needs. The situation is described in very similar terms to that of the Tree of Knowledge in Genesis: man may eat of all the fruits in the
garden save for those of this tree, a law given not out
of perversity on the part of God, but for man's protection.

Within the bounds of 'das Entsetzliche' come all the
apparently meaningless disasters which befall man, such
as wars, floods, shipwrecks and earthquakes - the dark
side of life discussed in Chapter Two and which Usinger

regards as part of a long-term plan of which man is ignorant:

> Es muß das
> Schiff zerschellen am
> Kap der guten Hoffnung,
> Daß eine Blume das Haupt
> Hebe aus ewigem Schnee. (46)

To the angel, who can view things from the standpoint of eternity, 'das Entsetzliche' and 'das Liebliche' are both seen as purely functional: the concession which he makes to man, preventing him from dwelling on the dark side of life, is equally functional, for without it all human life would cease.

While Hagen regards the 'späte Nymphen' as the culminating achievement of Usinger's mythology, Michel regards the 'Engel der Vergessenheit' as his most significant creation:

> Daß Usinger diesen Engel zu Gesicht bekam und ihn
> als 'ältester Geist der Welt' in die Schar der
> waltenden Götter einreihte, ist vielleicht die
> tiefsinnigste Leistung seines mythischen Denkens.
> Sie hat mythenschöpferische Bedeutung. (47)

The angel is closely allied to the force of love, and its powers of consolation are envisaged as the sole means of countering despair. It is the only permanent proof of the existence of a 'divine Grace' directed towards man:

> Engel, licht auf lichtem Himmelsringe,
> Flügelregend stehn die hohen Worte,
> Zugeordnet jedes seinem Dinge,
> Liebe-blickend nach dem irdischen Orte.
>
> Plötzlich stürzt es blitzend steil auf Schwingen
> In die Tiefe, wo die Rufe wären.
> Ewige Einung soll noch nicht gelingen.
> Nur ein Kuß. Doch tönen alle Sphären. (48)

Not only the 'Engel der Vergessenheit' but also all other angels are part of the cosmic force of love; each angel has its allocated function and duties with regard to earthly life. They cannot grant man 'ewige Einung', but their kiss, a token of the love they represent, provides an intimation of cosmic harmony.

In Gesichter und Gesichte, Usinger includes a short essay on 'Die Engel', which is revealing not only with regard to his concept of the angels, but also for his mythology as a whole. 'Es gibt sie und es gibt sie nicht', he begins.(49) Space probes have as yet encountered no angels floating about the cosmos; the reason that man envisages them so doing is the close association between angels and God, what Usinger terms 'das Immer-bei-Gott-Sein'. Elsewhere he writes: 'Es gibt keine Engel ohne Gott. Daher entspricht auch jeder Engel seinem Gott'.(50) Since God is no longer confined to some heavenly region of light, it follows that the angels too - as His representatives - have changed their place of abode.

Although Usinger insists that the powers represented by God and the gods precede man's awareness of them, the precise form which these powers assume is still within man's control. Usinger discards the idea of a hierarchy of angels in which some are superior to others on the grounds that the divine cannot change its essence, only its manner of communication. The position of each angel, according to Usinger, is determined by this manner of communication: 'Wie der Engel das Heilige darstellt und wieder aus sich ausstrahlt, das bestimmt seinen Rang'.(51)

Each angel, then, depicts 'das Heilige' in its own way, and it is artists and sculptors who have given physical form to these forces or spirits. To Usinger their work, like that of the poet, is a demonstration of the artist's desire to transform the world into a higher reality or 'heaven'. Usinger himself has accumulated a large collection of statues of angels and saints, and on occasion he refers to them in his poems:

> Die immer schwermütigen Heiligen
> Und die heiteren Engel,
> Die Madonnen mit schön gerafften
> Gewändern. Sie blicken

An dir vorbei in den großen Raum der Welt,
Der ihrer Hilfe bedarf. (52)

The angels direct their attention not towards individuals,
but towards the earth as a whole, which Usinger considers
to be greatly in need of their assistance. They are no
longer messengers of direct divine intervention, in contrast to biblical days, but, as representatives of love,
indicate the only way in which man can create the 'heaven'
towards which he aspires: 'Die Welt ist ein angefangener
und nicht zu Ende gekommener Himmel. Und dafür sind uns
diese unzähligen Engel ein Zeichen'.(53) Although God
Himself has disappeared completely from man's view, He
has left behind Him the angels as witnesses of His divinity. The features of the angels are devised by man,
yet Usinger believes they have a reality of their own
which is communicated through man, but is 'etwas ganz
anderes, Mächtigeres, Bleibenderes'(54) than anything
which man could create.

In one of his most recent poems Usinger ridicules
any assertion that angels are a mere superstition and
do not really exist:

Die Welt ist voll von Engeln. Die Welt wimmelt von Engeln.
Jeden Tag begegnest du ihnen,
Aber du erkennst sie nicht.
...
Gäbe es nicht so viele Engel auf der Welt, sie hätte
Sich selbst schon aus der Welt des Löwen aufgefressen.
Aber so lebt sie,
Ärmlich genug, mit ihren Resten an Engeln,
Den unerkannten. (55)

The angel is needed as an antidote to the evil which man
has brought into the world: the angel can save the earth
from the imminent catastrophe with which it is threatened.
Although Usinger does not believe the angel could ever
bridge the gulf which surrounds man and separates him
from God, he regards the angel as a sympathetic link between man and the intangible forces which surround him,
a source of comfort which can help man both to endure the

physical void around the earth and to fill the spiritual
one.
Usinger frequently finds evidence of angelic forces in
human beings. Hagen writes:

> Usinger hat in der Güte und Lauterkeit, die ihm in
> einigen Freunden, Männern und Frauen, begegnet ist,
> stets das Engelhafte gesehen, eine Verkörperung
> dessen, was er in der Welt an Engelhaften wirksam
> wußte.(56)

One such person was Usinger's close friend Hans Arp:

> Ich habe Usinger von Arp, wann immer das Gespräch
> auf ihn kam, mir der größten Verehrung, ja Liebe
> sprechen hören, und nie unterließ er, das Angelische
> im Wesen Arps zu erwähnen.(57)

Usinger attributes to an angelic force within Arp the
strength to overcome the suffering caused not only by
the general state of the world and the apparent ineffectiveness of art, but also by the death of Arp's
mother in 1930 and of his wife Sophie Täuber in 1943.
Even when the angelic forces are less evident, Usinger
can still exhort man not to despair; help is always at
hand for those who seek it:

> Verzweifle nicht,
> Wenn kein Engel zu dir kommt.
> Gott selbst kommt zu dir,
> Unsichtbar, ohne Wort,
> Wenn du ihn rufst,
> Eine Gewißheit, inwendig. (58)

If all intermediary methods of communication fail, man
still has the hope of a direct, intuitive contact with
the divinity.
Usinger's 'God', then, is neither a personal God nor
a God of salvation, but a God of creation scarcely to be
distinguished from the Logos, which does not exist 'above'
the world but is in the world and inseparable from it.
The gods, as Usinger sees them, represent various aspects

of the Logos - Apollo its ability to give order and form,
Aphrodite the concept of beauty, Dionysus the sensual
and chaotic elements, the nymphs Nature's perfection, and
so on - but none of these gods are concerned directly
with man. Usinger, as a poet, may appeal to Apollo or
Aphrodite and even feel their presence from time to time,
but the effort is all on his part. The gods may need
man in order to give physical form to the spiritual concepts which they represent, but they have no means of
alleviating his suffering. Christianity is far more
concerned with this aspect of existence. The Logos is
essentially a creative force, but Usinger combines with
it the force of 'Liebe', which likewise permeates the
whole of existence. Christ was the initiator of this
concept of love, and although Usinger sometimes attributes to other 'Götter' a love of man, it is the Christian symbols of Christ and the angels which are its
clearest manifestation. The angels differ from the
gods, then, in that they have man's interests at heart,
or rather are invested with powers to counter man's
despair. Usinger's concept of the angel holds a unique
position in his philosophy in that it constitutes a
means of saving man from the silent abyss.

In general terms, Usinger's mythological creatures
represent suitable labels to attach to concepts which
are, Usinger admits, beyond the power of words - thus
it is that the Logos is described as a rustling, a
whisper, as music, or even as silence. Usinger's mythology is mid-way between the allegorical gods of Schiller
or Goethe and the actual natural forces or elements in
which Hölderlin believed. Usinger regards the gods as
intermediaries through whom mankind may ultimately be
restored to the close relationship with God which once
existed: 'Wir kommen nur über die Wirklichkeit und ihre
Götter zu Gott zurück'.(59) It should be noted that
Usinger refers to the gods as part of 'reality', for he
considers ideas to be just as much a part of the real
world as physical forms. In Medusa he writes:

Es ist sonderbar, daβ im Verlauf der menschlichen
Begriffsentwicklung der Begriff der Wirklichkeit
dazu gelangt ist, nur die irdische Dingwelt zu
meinen als jenes Erfahrungsbereich, in dem sich
der menschlichen Wahrnehmung und Erkenntnis ein
Da-Sein von unwiderleglicher Deutlichkeit offen-
bart. Der Geist aber, der dieses Da-Sein fest-
stellt, hat nicht soviel Gewiβheit seiner selbst,
nicht soviel Vertrauen in sich selbst, daβ er
das gleiche Maβ von 'Wirklichkeit' sich zuzusprech-
en unternähme.(60)

Usinger believes that spiritual concepts have just as
much 'reality' as the more concrete areas of experience,
and that myths and fairy-tales, which seem so far removed from everyday life, are just as much a part of
life as factual reports in newspapers. The myth may
appear to be an assemblage of improbable events, but,
by defining man's relationship to his environment in
the form of allegory and symbolism, the myth, like the
biblical parable, has an enduring relevance beyond the
reach of purely factual accounts. The myth knows no
sequence of time, only an eternal present. So the
'myth' is in many respects more realistic than so-called
'facts' because it is the product of a creative imagination which reflects man's hopes, fears and beliefs
about the nature of the world.

NOTES

1. Letter 64 (10.5.73).
2. Usinger, Welt ohne Klassik, Darmstadt, 1960, p.61.
3. Letter 62 (6.4.73).
4. Usinger, Das Wort, p.70.
5. Usinger, Hermes, p.22.
6. Usinger, Merkbücher, pp.99-100.
7. Usinger, Die Stimmen, p.100.
8. Usinger, Die Stimmen, p.100.
9. Usinger, Der Stern Vergeblichkeit, p.117.

10. Usinger, Galaxis, pp.31-32.
11. Usinger, Die Geheimnisse, p.61.
12. Usinger, Der Stern Vergeblichkeit, p.30.
13. S. Hagen, Fritz Usinger, Endlichkeit und Unendlich-keit, Bonn, 1972, p.113.
14. Usinger, Das Wort, p.88.
15. Usinger, Die Geheimnisse, p.13.
16. See C. R. Barker, 'Fritz Usinger: Poet, Essayist and Critic', pp.194-200.
17. Usinger, Das Wort, p.21.
18. Usinger, Die Stimmen, p.97.
19. Usinger, Gedanken, unpaginated.
20. Letter 59 (7.3.73).
21. See Hagen: 'Im Bild des Gottes Apollon ist der Logos Gestalt geworden, die Wahrheit als Schönheit in Er-scheinung getreten'. op.cit., p.107.
22. Letter 59 (7.3.73).
23. M. Grant, Myths of the Greeks and Romans, London, 1962, p.52.
24. Usinger, Das Wort, p.91.
25. Usinger, Die Stimmen, p.59.
26. Usinger, Die Stimmen, p.61.
27. Usinger, Die Stimmen, p.65.
28. Usinger, Das Wort, p.39.
29. Usinger, Das Wort, p.38-39.
30. The powers of petrification attributed to Medusa prompt Usinger to name after her a collection of essays about sculpture: Medusa, Dessau, 1940.
31. Usinger, Medusa, p.60.
32. Usinger, Die Stimmen, p.84.
33. ibid.
34. Usinger, Die Stimmen, p.85.
35. See Chapter Two, p.33.
36. Usinger, Die Stimmen, p.81.
37. ibid.
38. Usinger, Das Wort, p.72.
39. Usinger, Canopus, pp.16-17.
40. Interview, August, 1972.
41. Usinger, Der Stern Vergeblichkeit, pp.90-91.

42. Usinger, Die Geheimnisse, p.42.
43. H. A. Seelbach, Dichtung und Weltbild Fritz Usingers, Bad Nauheim, 1948.
44. Usinger, Die Geheimnisse, p.42.
45. Usinger, Die Stimmen, p.90.
46. Usinger, Die Stimmen, p.92.
47. W. Michel, 'Über Fritz Usinger', Der Bücherwurm, Leipzig, 1942, Vol.8, pp.135-42.
48. Usinger, Die Stimmen, p.30.
49. Usinger, Gesichter und Gesichte, p.115.
50. Usinger, Medusa, p.58.
51. Usinger, Gesichter und Gesichte, p.115.
52. Usinger, Der Planet, p.57.
53. Usinger, Gesichter und Gesichte, p.116.
54. Usinger, Gesichter und Gesichte, p.115.
55. Usinger, Galaxis, p.52.
56. Hagen, op.cit., p.176.
57. Hagen, op.cit., p.224.
58. Usinger, Der Planet, p.91.
59. Usinger, Merkbücher, p.33.
60. Usinger, Medusa, p.51.

CHAPTER 5

COSMOLOGY

Throughout his life, Usinger has been concerned with the cosmos as a whole, and it should be emphasised that his interest is by no means confined to realms of experience relating to the imagination or to the age-old beliefs and symbols discussed in the two foregoing chapters. The scientific developments of recent years and their repercussions with regard to the role of mankind in general and the artist in particular have long been a subject of fascination for him. Looking at the history of cosmology, Usinger expresses surprise at finding how small a part discoveries as revolutionary as those of Copernicus in the sixteenth century have played in European literature. Even the great Goethe, he points out, for all his interest in science, practically disregarded the existence of other planets and intergalactic space and continued instead to postulate the belief in Nature's protective and life-supporting role which had dominated previous centuries. Usinger considers the sense of security which such a position inspires to be totally false for mankind and one which it is impossible to maintain in the present age, where the greater part of the universe is known to be inimical to life as it has developed on the planet earth.

In his essay 'Tellurische und planetarische Dichtung', Usinger takes man to task for his indifference towards an area of experience which, whether he is aware of it or not, has the most critical impact on his daily life:

Es ist eine psychologisch merkwürdige Angelegenheit, daß die kosmischen Einsichten in die Unendlichkeit des Weltraums, in seine Mittelpunktlosigkeit und die daraus sich ergebende völlig exzentrische Stellung der Erde schon uralt sind, ohne sich dem menschlichen Bewußtsein deutlicher anzuprägen. Der Mensch hat an diese für ihn schwer zu verarbeitenden Einsichten einfach vorbeigedacht, so als ob es sie gar nicht gäbe. (1)

Usinger maintains that intellectual progress in the nine-
teenth and twentieth centuries has been confined to scientific thinkers; in the literary world, the planets outside
the earth simply furnish imagery with which to adorn poetry
and fiction, nothing more. The human personality and man's
immediate social environment remain a dominant theme for
creative literature, which acts as if the earth were immune
from any external influences. Usinger does not suggest that
the writer should cease to concern himself with man's position, but simply that it should be seen within the wider
context of the entire complex of cosmic forces by which man
is surrounded and influenced.

Even in an area like science fiction which has the
opportunity of ranging beyond the immediate individual and
social problems that preoccupy Western literature, the interest in the wider cosmos is more apparent than real. The
exotic setting is generally a mere backcloth telling us
nothing of the real nature of outer space, and the 'monsters'
which inhabit the world of science fiction are, in the words
of Michel Butor, 'despite their crests, their tentacles,
their scales, ... much less different from the average
American than an ordinary Mexican'.(2) Where science fiction
does have a serious purpose - in the works of Huxley and
Orwell, for example - it is as a form of social criticism,
that is, precisely the field which in Usinger's view leads
away from the larger issues. By transposing existing values
to a different, more exotic background in order to satirise
them, science fiction of this type merely extends the prevailing tendencies of twentieth-century literature towards
social comment without capturing anything of the real essence of outer space.

One of the few exceptions to the general lack of interest
in cosmology on the part of creative writers is Alfred Mombert, whom Usinger hails as the first European poet to
extend his sphere of interest to the whole cosmos; he calls
him 'der erste deutsche Weltraumdichter':(3)

Er hatte als erster in einer plötzlichen Eröffnung des
Gefühls die Existenz des Kosmos erfahren und zwar als
eine Existenz, die uns ganz nahe, bis auf die Haut nahe

gerückt ist. Er hatte als erster die Welt nicht nur
als ein tellurisches, sondern als ein planetarisches
Ereignis erlebt.(4)

Mombert's poems, or rather cycles of poems, are centred not
on the earth but on the cosmos in its entirety. They show
man coming to terms with this cosmos, a process which,
although inevitably viewed from the human standpoint, is
seen only partly from the earth and partly from points in
space outside the earth, in the depths of the infinite
cosmos. The earth is not the centre of life in Mombert's
poetry, merely one planet amongst countless others. Never-
theless, it has a special significance as the home of human
culture and philosophy, even when the creative spirit which
has produced this culture moves on to other areas of the
cosmos, as it does in Mombert's poems, for the rest of the
known universe has no parallel culture:

> Der außerirdische Weltraum ist noch nicht menschlich
> durchdrungen. Diese Aufgabe, wie eng oder weit man sie
> auch fassen mag, bleibt dem Menschen noch zu lösen.
> Wieviel seiner Zukunft er darauf wird verwenden müssen,
> wissen wir nicht. Wir wissen auch nicht, ob ihm über-
> haupt eine wenn auch noch so relative Lösung dieser
> Aufgabe gelingen wird. Alfred Mombert ist der einzige
> Dichter, der alle diese Zusammenhänge sah.(5)

Mombert has no fear of the infinitude of the universe,
largely because he views it purely imaginatively. The same
idealism which prevented Mombert from acknowledging the
perils of his position as a Jew in Nazi Germany until his
arrest in 1940 also prevailed in his view of the cosmos:

> Es ist als spräche hier gar nicht der Mensch Alfred
> Mombert, sondern ein mythisches Ich, das mit viel
> gewältigeren Kräften ausgestattet ist als die Seele
> eines Menschen. ... Ein Gott könnte nicht viel anders
> dieser Welt begegnen. Mombert sieht den Kosmos mythisch,
> nicht realistisch. Die Kräfte des Weltalls formen sich
> ihm zu personalen Gestalten mit Bewußtsein und Sprache.
> ... Das Weltall wird noch aus der Ferne des Geistes

gesehen und nicht etwa aus der Nähe des Weltraum-
schiffs.(6)

Although Usinger too endeavours to render the invisible
cosmic forces at least imaginatively accessible to man,
he views outer space essentially not as a mythical realm,
but as a physical reality. This, in his opinion, Mombert
does not do. The awesome nature of the silent cosmic void -
which Usinger himself feels very keenly - is dispelled for
Mombert by the creations of his own imagination. Although
he realises that human values have a limited range and
applicability, Mombert's mythical figures, like the Greek
gods, have certain similarities with mankind which mitigate
their remoteness in other respects.

Usinger's interest in cosmology can be traced back to his
first contact with Mombert's poetry when a schoolboy of
seventeen and is reflected in his own poetry and essays
from that time onwards. Initially this interest, like
Mombert's, was subjective rather than scientific, and is
incorporated into Usinger's poetry as one of many other
elements. This is the case in Der ewige Kampf, where
Usinger writes in the 'Vierzeiler' which terminate this
volume:

> Es formt mein Geist die Mond- und Sternenheere,
> die kleine Erde und den weiten Raum,
> und füllt mit Seligkeit die große Leere
> in einem ungeheuren Traum.(7)

The imaginative nature of this early expression of Usinger's
cosmic awareness can be seen from its designation as a
'Traum'. Usinger's first preoccupations were his own
poetic self, earthly Nature, and the relationship between
the two. His conviction that he has a 'mission' as a poet
comes at a relatively early stage, and is seen as part of
a comprehensive scheme of creative forces, in which the
concept of the Logos plays a major role. Until the late
'thirties, however, these forces are seen purely in their
relationship to man and Nature on earth, not to the rest of
the cosmos. In Das Wort, for example, the word 'Unendlichkeit', so frequent in Usinger's later work, occurs only

once. Only in <u>Die Geheimnisse</u> in 1937 does the first
real break come with traditional religion and the Christian conception of God. This, we have seen, is accompanied
by speculative, abstract poetry, which branches out into
alchemy and medieval philosophy.

It is the essay-collection <u>Geist und Gestalt</u>, published
in 1939, which marks the beginning of the general revision
of values which accompanies Usinger's increasing involve-
ment in cosmology. The essay 'Unendlichkeit und Gestalt',
as its title indicates, examines the significance of infinity for earthly forms, man included. From the time of
Ancient Greece to the present century, man has been
the focal point for all metaphysical and morphological
speculations. In the belief that he was the culmination
of creation, all religions and philosophies centred
around him, and everything else was allocated a subordinate
position. Usinger points out that science has made it
increasingly obvious that the world's forces are not directed towards man, nor do they act in his interests:

> Wir wissen, die Kräfte meinen uns nicht mehr, oder sie
> meinen uns nur genau so weit, wie sie alles Stoff- und
> Gestalt-gewordene meinen.(8)

Man cannot control natural forces; the most he can hope to
achieve is to adapt some of them to his own use by construct-
ing machines and instruments which act in accordance with
natural laws. The discovery that the universe is so vast
as to be to all intents and purposes infinite constitutes
the final blow to any pretensions man may still entertain
about his own situation:

> Wir sehen auf die Welt nicht mehr mit dem ruhigen
> Blick des Besitzenden, sondern mit dem suchenden Blick
> des Bedürftigen, des Enterbten gar oder Betrogenen, der
> den Verlust seiner Teilhabe niemals verschmerzen kann.(9)

Any sense of security regarding man's situation in the
cosmos is, in Usinger's view, entirely without foundation.

For Usinger, the concept of infinity implies the total
isolation of man. Unable to reconcile any idea of a per-

sonal or loving God with an infinite, 'inhuman' universe,
Usinger sees man as 'lost', for there is no hierarchy of
existence in which he has an assigned place and function.
The validity of any religious or philosophical hierarchy is
weakened beyond recall when confronted by the prospect of
an infinity of time and space:

> So relativiert sich alles, das Vergängliche vor der
> Unendlichkeit der Zeit und das 'nahezu' Unvergängliche
> vor der Unendlichkeit des Raumes. Es ist die Position
> der Positionslosigkeit, die Existenz der Existenz-
> losigkeit. (10)

Whilst adhering to the belief that microcosm and macro-
cosm are governed by the same laws, Usinger emphasises that
there is now no doubt that it is man who is dependent on
the rest of the cosmos and not vice versa.

We have seen that Usinger believes the universe to be
a complex system of interrelated forces, both 'positive'
and 'negative', which together maintain the existence of
the world and lend it meaning. From the point of view of
his philosophy, perhaps the most significant scientific
discovery of recent times is Einstein's theory of rela-
tivity. As the interrelationship of mass and energy
abolishes any clear division between material reality and
intangible cosmic forces (seemingly adding support to
Usinger's alchemical theories), and as the time-space con-
tinuum eliminates the 'absolute' value of time or space,
so Usinger regards any system of thought which relies upon
absolutes as both outmoded and unrealistic.

In the introduction to his latest volume of aphorisms,
Merkbücher, he suggests that the deeper man probes into
the mysteries of the universe, the more mysterious they
become:

> Die Wissenschaft, besonders die Naturwissenschaft
> unseres Jahrhunderts, hat ungeheure Funde der Erkennt-
> nis erschlossen und ist damit zu dem Ergebnis gelangt,
> daß die Welt dadurch für uns nur noch rätselhafter
> geworden ist. (11)

It is, he says, as if the essential mystery were continually receding from our grasp.

It is this essential mystery which so intrigues Usinger, who has described himself as a 'Rätseljäger'. No philosophy or religion can ever offer more than a partial explanation, since 'God', whom he equates with the 'Welträtsel',(12) has deliberately withdrawn from the world, leaving behind Him an infinite Nature with which man can never fully come to terms:

> Eine der schwierigsten Aufgaben menschlicher Erfahrung
> ist es, den Alltag zu begreifen als absichtliche Ver-
> borgenheit Gottes. Die Dichter wissen noch etwas vom
> wahren Leben, aber auch nur blaβe Abglänze, matte
> Ahnungen.(13)

God no longer has a special relationship with mankind. He is utterly remote from man and, like the depths of the cosmos, completely unaffected by anything that man may do.

While the French philosopher Blaise Pascal in the seventeenth century was able to regard the Christian God as the only means of saving man from the cold and silent infinity of Nature, Usinger, who shares Pascal's horror of such an unresponsive universe, identifies God with this infinity. Like the universe itself, God is self-sufficient in His infinity and has no real conception of the restricted existence which man leads. Usinger's God becomes a 'Deus Immutabilis':

> Der du, verändernd, dich nicht änderst,
> Ein All, erfüllt von ewigem Vollzug,
> Noch mit Unendlichem umränderst,
> Dahin kein Blick das Maβ des Menschen trug.
> ...
> Zeit ist kein Wort auf jenen höchsten Sitzen
> Noch Wandel dem, das aus sich selber stammt. (14)

Although the constituent elements of the universe undergo changes from time to time, these are not dependent on the actions of mankind, nor do they affect the overall composition of the cosmos:

'Ich bin nicht das ewig anders. Ich wohne nicht hinter
                                      Wolken.
...
Ich bin all-alles Sein. Ich überlebe meine Zerstörungen.
Wer wollte die Unendlichkeit zerstören?' (15)

These last words are spoken by the 'one remaining God' in a
collection of poems entitled <u>Niemandsgesang</u>, written by
Usinger during the 'fifties, at a time when the full impact
of man's cosmic isolation caused him to revise completely
his views on natural and artistic form which had centred
on Goethe's morphology.

With this growing awareness of the comparative insignificance of all earthly forms, artistic form included,
Usinger's poetry enters an entirely new phase; both form
and content mark a break with his previous style. Of the
volume <u>Niemandsgesang</u>, published in 1957, Usinger says:

> Was vorher unter den Aspekten Goethes noch ein
> 'Jemand' war, der ist nun unter dem kosmischen
> Aspekt ein 'Niemand' geworden, und der in diesem
> Gedichtband spricht, das ist eigentlich ein Nie-
> mand, der nun zufälligerweise noch sprechen kann,
> noch Worte hat, aber in seiner Rangordnung in der
> Welt ist er eben ein Niemand, und dieses ganze
> Buch sind Gesänge eines Niemands, d.h. eines Wesens,
> das eigentlich überhaupt nicht existiert, sobald
> man es im Hinblick auf die Gesamtheit ansieht. (16)

Despite a mood of despondency in regard both to man's position in the cosmos and to the futility of his own actions,
Usinger, as Hagen points out, is never nihilistic:

> Usinger behauptet niemals die Sinnlosigkeit des
> Seins, wohl aber nun die Sinnlosigkeit des Sagens,
> die den Nihilisten nicht einfällt:
>
> > Gott will allein sein.
> > Beuge dich!
> > Schweige. (17)

Despite the lack of rhyme and form, and the apparent dis-
integration of Usinger's poetic style, Hagen sees in this

volume an unconscious 'new beginning', poems dependent not on rhyme or regular metre but sustained by their imagery and their own rhythms. The poems in this collection are certainly amongst Usinger's most forceful, despite the fact that negative elements in the vocabulary, always a predilection with Usinger, become more prevalent than ever.

The word 'niemand' assumes a particular importance. The deliberate ambiguity of the term is evident: man, like all earthly forms, exists and yet does not exist. To borrow an expression from Pascal, he is 'un néant à l'égard de l'infini, un tout à l'égard du néant'.(18) Similarly, Usinger refers to himself as a 'Bienenkönig':

> Es gibt ihn nicht, den Bienenkönig,
> Und dennoch bin ich es: ein Bienenkönig.
> Stets schon war ich der, den es nicht gibt,
> Und ich werde es immer sein. (19)

His actual nature has not changed: he is still a poet collecting 'den Nektar verschwundener Götter den niemand mehr trinken will',(20) but his individual insignificance in earthly terms has become synonymous with non-existence in cosmic terms. In a subsequent collection, Usinger also applies the term 'niemand' to intergalactic space. Here, instead of a 'Bienenkönig, den es nicht gibt' is a 'niemand, den es doch gar nicht gibt':

> Er ist natürlich überall,
> Und er ist unberechenbar.(21)

Man's fear of this 'niemand' is a fear of the unknown, because it cannot be comprehended by human logic:

> Er geht nicht. Er hat es nicht nötig.
> Er kann sein, wo er will,
> Rasch wie der Gedanke.
> Er ist rascher als dein Blick.
> Er kann auch langsamer sein. (22)

The 'niemand' cannot be measured in human terms, for his mode of existence is so utterly alien to any form of earthly life that no meaningful comparison can be established.

Man's material substantiality is itself at variance with
the prevailing nature of the cosmos, which is largely composed of force-fields invisible to man.

The human frame of reference can no longer have any
pretension to universality, man is no longer the measure
of all things, for it appears that the human element has
been excluded from the rest of the cosmos:

> Das Menschliche ist verloren gegangen.
> Das Unmenschliche ist mit sich allein
> Und spricht seine Sprache der Wortlosigkeit.(23)

Usinger, as a poet, is particularly disconcerted by the
silence of the cosmos. In his _Gedanken_ he writes: 'Wäre
es nicht noch viel furchtbarer, wenn die donnernden
Stürze des Niagara oder Sambesi völlig lautlos fielen? Aber
dies gibt es längst. Es ist der Katarakt der Zeit'.(24)
Temporal and spatial infinity are equally silent and incomprehensible to man, whose words and actions are lost
in the void:

> Von Welt zu Welt führt nur
> Pfadloser Abgrund.
> Von Herz zu Herz nur
> Pfadloser Abgrund.
> Alle Musiken habe ich entfesselt,
> Sie füllen den Raum nicht.
> Kein Ton tötet je das Schweigen.
> Keine Zärtlichkeit durchhaucht je die Kälte,
> Die Liebenden haben vergeblich geliebt.(25)

The cold, silent emptiness of the cosmos also enters the
realm of love. The only chance of escaping total isolation is in a relationship with another person who will,
through her love, make bearable a world too bleak to face
alone. This escape reveals itself as illusory, however,
for even love is incapable of compensating for man's soli-
tary position in the universe and is itself without hope
of fulfilment: 'Einen Menschen lieben: das ist so wie wenn
einer eine Quelle durch Umarmung festhalten wollte'.(26)

A relationship based on enjoyment of the present moment
can never be satisfactory for Usinger, who feels his mission
is eternal; a lasting relationship, however, rendered sufficiently difficult by his devotion to his work and by
man's constantly changing nature, becomes impossible in
an infinite world, where it is beset by an unending suc-
cession of problems which the entire lifetime of a human
being is insufficient to resolve. 'Die Liebe', says
Usinger, is 'unvollendbar'.(27) The infinity of the universe reflects upon all 'finite' values and relationships
because of the different pressures and problems which
existence in such a world entails. Not only is love itself
incapable of reaching a state of complete fulfilment, it
is also unable to bring about any long-term amelioration
in the situations with which it comes into contact:

> Die Liebe vollendet nichts.
> Sie ist voll wunderbarer Anfänge, aber das
> Unendliche überwältigt sie.
> Sie verliert sich in den Weiten der Welt'.(28)

The optimistic beginnings initiated by love are swamped
by the daunting prospect of infinity; in an infinite
world nothing is 'vollendbar', for there is no possibility
of perfection in a universe where every supposedly completed process can be superseded by another:

> Eure Liebe schenkt ihr dem Abgrund,
> Der alles verschlingt und vergißt.
> Eure Herzen schenkt ihr der Nacht, die sie
> hinwegnimmt,
> Euer Teil ist Zerfall, Abbruch, Trümmerstätte,
> Wind über Gräbern.(29)

The mere presence of the void, which constitutes most of
the universe, invalidates human emotions and further
emphasises man's insignificance.

Since the void is a physical as well as a spiritual
phenomenon, man has no hope of ever banishing it completely:

> Es ist die Welt zu groß geworden,
> Ein Abgrund der Abgründe.

Wohin du schaust, ergreift dich
Schwindel vor der Tiefe.
Was du sprichst, entfernt sich weltwärts
Und schwindet hinter den kühlen
Planeten-Feuer. Niemals führt
Ein Steig dorthin.
Die Welt ist ohne Wege.(30)

Even the positive, creative act of the poet seems at times irrelevant, for although it may overcome some of the spiritual barriers which separate man from his origins, it can achieve nothing in physical terms:

Schütte die Gedichte in den Abgrund!
Horche hinab!
Niemals hörst du sie auffallen.
Das Bodenlose gibt keine Antwort.
Was nicht geschaffen ist, zu empfangen,
Kennt keinen Dank.(31)

While Usinger continues to believe in the fundamental unity of all experience, he acknowledges that nothing man can do will ever fully restore this sense of unity, which seems forever lost in the vastness of a spatial and temporal infinity. No human activity or emotion, even love, can affect the impersonal silence of the cosmos.

However, Usinger does not assume an entirely negative and pessimistic stance with regard to love; instead of renouncing it, he turns the infinity of the cosmos to good account by embracing a concept of love in which fulfilment is not the prime objective. The despondency of Niemandsgesang yields place to a determination to make the best of the situation in Der Stern Vergeblichkeit:

Ich weiß, daß alles in der Welt einander fremd
                                         ist.
Dies ist kein Grund gegen das Leben.
...
Lebe, als ob die Welt wahr wäre,
Lebe, als ob die Liebe wahr wäre.(32)

This encapsulates what is henceforth to be Usinger's philosophy of life, and, developing the notion of 'Vergeblichkeit' discussed in the preceding chapter, where Christ's message of universal love was accepted as a principle despite its apparent ineffectiveness, Usinger advocates the idea of a 'cosmic' love. This is a love which extends beyond any human being into the depths of the cosmos:

> eine Umarmung
> Weit über die Geliebte hinaus,
> Deren du dich kaum noch erinnerst,
> Eine Umarmung der Welt.(33)

The most significant feature of this love is that it is without any hope of response:

Eine solche Liebe ist ohne Erwiderung, denn der Gegenstand dieser Liebe ist, wie der Gedichtschluß sagt:

> Ein Ungeheuer aus Feuer und Eis,
> grausam, maßlos, rasend, diese deine
> Liebe, fortstürzend, unnahbar.

Denn diese Galaxien stürzen ja mit ungeheuerlicher Geschwindigkeit von dem menschlichen Liebenden hinweg.(34)

Far from answering man's attempts to come to terms with them, the galaxies appear to be moving away from him with ever-increasing velocity, and the concept of love is meaningless to them:

> Es wird die Liebe nicht geliebt.
> Welt weiß nicht, daß es Liebe gibt.
> Das Wort ist ein verlorner Stern
> Im Abgrund des verlornen Herrn.(35)

Yet, if love is to retain its validity as a universal force, it must reach out even to those parts of the cosmos which are unaware of its very existence. Usinger envisages invisible threads or light-rays emanating from love to unite the multifarious forms and forces extant in the universe:

> Und dennoch schwebt die Welt im Wort.
> Unsichtbar Fäden hier und dort
> Verbinden, was sich niemals kennt
> Und niemals sich mit Namen nennt.
>
> Die Liebe nur, sie sucht und sinnt,
> Was sich an Himmelszeichen spinnt:
> Ein Lichtgeweb aus Süd und Nord
> Bis an des Raumes tiefsten Bord.

It is Usinger's persistent faith in the unifying 'Liebe-Wort' or Logos which gives him the incentive to pursue a goal which by its very nature is beyond all hope of attainment.

In one of his most significant collections of poetry, Canopus, (1968), the star Canopus, which the Americans have used as a navigational fixed point for their space-flights, symbolises the goal in the outer regions of the cosmos towards which man must strive, despite the absence of response:

> in der Weltnacht steht
> Ein Silberblick, mit Namen Canopus, der bannt
> dich,
> Auch wenn du niemals
> An seinen kraterstarrenden Gestaden landest.(36)

Canopus, emanating its rays from some distant part of the universe, a spark of light against the blackness of the 'Weltnacht', is the glimmer of truth, of meaning, towards which Usinger is striving in order to illumine the dark-ness and confusion of our own world:

> Es gibt nur ihn für dich und nur die
> Richtung auf ihn, dir wohl ein Ziel,
> Doch keine Ankunft.(37)

In 'Ort der Orte', Usinger calls Canopus 'das Unerreich-bare', 'die Unsichtbarkeit', 'das Unfindbare'; whatever his efforts he will never attain his distant goal:

in gleicher Ferne stets steht Canopus.

The star shines above, a guiding light, like the Star of
Bethlehem leading the Wise Men to Christ. Elsewhere,
Usinger speaks of a 'Fata Morgana, durch die man hindurch-
schreitet, ohne ihrer je lebhaft zu werden'.(38) Standing thus distantly out in space, Canopus represents God
or infinity. Usinger calls the star a lidless eye,
gazing steadfastly into the depths of the cosmos.

   In one of his latest poems, Usinger refers to man's
inbuilt need for some kind of goal, however distant and
intangible:

                    Dein
         Ganz will ein Ziel, und sei es
         Das allerfernste
         ...
         Du, grenzenloser Geist, suchst Grenzen, und
                                        lägen sie
         Am letzten Stern vor dem
         Noch ungeborenen Welt-Raum.(39)

Usinger regards the actual distance which separates man
from the rest of the cosmos as equivalent to the dimensions of the problems involved in its understanding.
Despite space-probes and the detailed scientific investigations of extra-terrestial bodies which they have made
possible, no real contact with the rest of the universe
will ever be established, Usinger maintains, for the very
nature of these planets as well as their distance from
the earth constitutes an insurmountable obstacle. Never-
theless, he believes that a kind of compromise is possible.
Although there is no chance of attaining full knowledge
or understanding of the universe, nor of achieving perfection in any realm of human experience, by continuing
to aim towards the stars man will become aware of his own
position with regard to these distant fellow-members of
his universe:

> ewig ohne Ankunft, Canopus,
> Doch immer auf den Weg zu dir.(40)

Aided by the powers of imagination and love, which
alone are able to transcend the limitations of a finite
world with finite values, man can extend his horizons
beyond the sphere of the known and familiar world into
infinity, into the realm of 'das Unvollendbare' and 'das
Vergebliche', yet without losing sight of earthly life.
In Der Sinn und das Sinnlose, Usinger writes: 'Die Wurzeln
der Materie sind die Wurzeln des Himmels'.(41) Although
the distant planets can never be reduced to the familiar
and manageable proportions of man's earthly surroundings,
Usinger is able to trace a path from earthly Nature at its
most basic level to Canopus and other remote regions of
the cosmos:

> es führt auch
> Der Weg vom Tal der Usa,
> Geheimen Wissens voll,
> Zum Cánopus-Gestirn im tiefsten Süden.
> Vom Dorf Mauswinkel führt ein Licht
> Zum Stern Atáir.
> Und überm Dorfe Schlechtenwegen fährt
> Der große Wagen mühlos seine goldne Bahn,
> Auf ewigem Äther,
> Ewige Zeiten fort.(42)

The villages named in this poem are all to be found in
the area around Usinger's home town of Friedberg, as is
the river Usa, from which his own family name is derived.
As their names suggest, the villages are remnants of a
primitive tradition which has largely become obscured
or overwhelmed by a materialist society; as such they are
symbolic of a basic and enduring quality which links
earthly life to that of the stars. Usinger comments
upon the mythical nature of the names given to the stars:

> Warum kann man einen Stern, ein Sternbild, eine
> Galaxie mit Namen wie Atair, Canopus, Leier, Argo

oder Andromeda benennèn, aber niemals mit dem
Namen Bismarck? Weil dahinter eine Einsicht in
den Rang von Weltstufen steht.(43)

The name Bismarck belongs to a particular era in man's
history and to a particular culture; the stars have no
such associations and are therefore accorded mythological
titles commensurate with their immortality. The names of
the outlying villages have a similar aura of myth, mystery
and timelessness, which links them to the stars and ini-
tiates a path towards them. This path, however, like
that depicted in Canopus, will never reach its goal.

Usinger's own particular role as a poet is part of
this 'mythologising' in the sense that he aspires to con-
dense life's essential truths into words, thereby render-
ing them immortal. In Das Wirkliche he describes the
poet's function as follows:

In Wort und Werk siegt der geisteserfüllte Augenblick über die unendlichen bewußtlosen Zeitläufe
der Natur. Der Geist faßt in einem Augenblick
Jahrmillionen bewußtlosen Werdens zusammen. Alles,
was geworden ist, tritt in ihn wie in einen Himmel
der Unsterblichkeit ein.(44)

While man himself is bound by many limitations, the human
mind is able to dispense with the restrictions of time
and space. Usinger allows his mind to explore the distant
regions of the cosmos in a number of poetry collections
which, like Canopus, bear titles closely corresponding
to his main preoccupations. After Der Stern Vergeblichkeit and Canopus, Usinger ventures imaginatively further
out into the cosmos, as is reflected by Der Planet (1972)
and Galaxis (1975). His latest volume of poetry, and
one of his most important to date, is shortly to appear
under the title Die himmlische Heimkehr (1976), where
Usinger depicts more vividly than ever before his visi-
onary experiences as a 'space-traveller' and his subsequent return to the earth.

In a stylistic tour de force, the three-part 'Huldigung für Dante', written in the rhyming tercets of the
Divine Comedy, Usinger pays tribute to his illustrious
predecessor who, like him, was concerned with presenting
a total and unified view of the universe. In physical
terms, however, the world which Usinger describes is the
converse of Dante's:

> Die Hölle über uns, die welten-große,
> Der Himmel irgendwo hinabgefallen
> Nicht mehr zu sehen in dem Urnacht-Schoße.

> Uns bleibt zu forschen, wie wir uns bei allen
> Welt-Wandlungen noch leidlich heil erhalten
> Und in die Ränder dieses Abgrunds krallen.(45)

While Dante's universe was a finite entity in which all
things had their allotted place, enabling him to become
'aller Welten höchster Meister',(46) the position of the
poet in the twentieth century is entirely different.
The universe has been discovered to be vast and impersonal,
utterly defeating the attempts of man to conquer it. The
written word has supremacy only in its power to crystal-
lise man's impressions of the universe and to render them
meaningful and enduring through the medium of imagery.
The poet must still aspire to convey a unified picture,
but it is a task which will never be completed. Usinger
describes the 'ewiges Werk' of the poet as

> Einheit zu schaffen, lebendiges, aus der
> Zahlosigkeit der
> Nicht-Zählbarkeiten.(47)

One essential feature of the universe as Usinger sees
it is the concept of the vortex which seems to govern all
planetary motion. The 'circular' structure of many of
Usinger's poems reflects this conception of the universe,
which is more prevalent than ever in Die himmlische
Heimkehr, where the 'Edda-Gesang' reflects a Nordic
belief in 'ewige Wiederkehr' similar to Usinger's own,
a belief in a universe constantly changing yet without

any apparent direction, 'die Wiederkehr ohne Wohin'.(48)
This circularity operates on both temporal and spatial
planes, for, as Einstein established, time and space are
really undivided:

> Die reine Zeit ist nichts als
> Der leere Raum, aus dem
> Alle Sterne hinweggefegt sind.
> Beide, Zeit und Raum, sind eines.(49)

Usinger conceives of time in visual terms, like the dome
of a giant cathedral in which individual events take place
as in a vast theatre. The curtain rises and falls as
specific episodes are played out. Numerical systems
devised by man have no connection with the real nature of
time, which forms an eternal backcloth to the vortex which
sweeps the earth in its path, together with all the other
planets, a

> himmlisch-höllischen Wirbel,
> Der lautlos über dir, unter dir tobt
> . Und dich mitreißt
> Durch die Äonen.(50)

Even the comets which do not orbit a sun are involved in
the circular motion of the universe as a whole. Whether
they will or no, human beings are caught up in this process, 'unauffindbar verloren'.
   Yet, despite the apparent random motion, the process
is in reality ordered and unified by 'God':

> Gott hütet seine Sonnen,
> Und kein Glitzerstern, kein
> Nachtschwarzer Dunkelstern
> Kann sich verlaufen. In
> Unsichtbaren Banden geht alles
> Vor und zurück,
> Hinauf und hinab.(51)

God is both silent and unattainable; He offers man no aid
in his path through the labyrinth, sending no Ariadne to

help him seek out the invisible threads, yet Usinger has
faith that there is a guiding principle which gives positive meaning to the whole of creation. There is no reason
why God should choose to reveal Himself to man, nor does
He do so; yet for those who have eyes to see, His eternal
presence is beyond dispute:

> Der Wind ist voll Weisheit für die Weisen.
> Für das Eulen-Auge ist die Nacht taghell.
> Die Sterne kreisen nicht im Leeren,
> Sondern sie sind gebunden in einem Geflecht
> Magischer Kräfte.
> ...
> Befeuert von Energien aus endloser Zeit
> ...
> Aber das alles ist deinen Augen nicht sicht-
> bar.(52)

The poet possesses special powers of perception which
enable him to see what others cannot. So it is that
Usinger's poems explore not only the 'visible' and'tangible' parts of the universe, but also the cosmic mysteries which constitute the essential core of all life:

> Innen ist mir ein
> Überwältigendes geschehen, das alles
> Irdische Tönen übertönt, für euch
> Lautlos und gar nicht
> Vernehmbar ...
> ... von einem
> Fernen Ozean der Wogen-Donner, der
> Unaufhaltsam die
> Aether-Räume durchbricht, aus
> Schwarzen Aeonen-Gründen
> Heraufsteigend mit Tausenden
> Silber- und Gold- und Feuerstimmen.(53)

Like Alfred Mombert, whom he so greatly admires, Usinger
has explored the very heart of creation, the source of
all energy. Instead of the 'light' which Usinger, fol-

lowing <u>Genesis</u>, generally associates with the creation of life, he now refers to the sound of 'Stern-Stimmen':

<blockquote>
so
Weht auch diese Ton-Woge
Der Billionen Stern-Stimmen,
Das sphärische Gefüge der
Welten-Fuge über mich
Hinweg, verborgenen
Räumen zu, jenseits
Des menschlichen Gehörs.(54)
</blockquote>

Like Mombert too, Usinger ultimately considers that the fitting abode for a creative poet is not in the inter-galactic 'ewig Gleiche', but on the planet earth, which alone is attuned to the outpourings of the human voice.

Usinger's awareness of the infinity of the cosmos increases his determination to translate ideas into poetic form, since for him, one of the greatest mira-cles is the way in which the creative energies of the universe assume the physical forms which we see on earth. This process Usinger regards as the sole concrete mani-festation of the mysterious 'God' who controls the threads which unify all cosmic life:

<blockquote>
Gott selbst ist immer unfindbar. Er teilt sich
uns nur mit in den Wundern seiner irdischen Ges-
taltbildung.(55)
</blockquote>

Usinger ends <u>Die himmlische Heimkehr</u> with the poet bow-ing before the rose, the 'Königin der Blumen',(56) which effortlessly and naturally creates beauty fit for the worship of its Maker. Usinger seeks to recapture this process with the written word and endeavours both to up-hold the value of earthly forms and to maintain his deep conviction that the human world is inextricably bound up with the fate of the rest of the cosmos. Out-lining in a recent letter the ultimate purpose of his life's work in general and of <u>Die himmlische Heimkehr</u> in particular, Usinger proposes the following solution to the problems which beset human existence in an 'inhuman' universe:

> Man kann nur auf der Erde, dieser lebendigen
> Gestalt-Welt, leben, aber immer hat man die
> unmenschliche Urwelt des Alls im Rücken, und
> kein Gedanke läßt sich denken, ohne daß man
> diesen Gedanken des Urweltschreckens mitdenkt.
> Dadurch fällt die menschliche Gedanken- und
> Werk-Welt nicht ins chaotische, sondern ganz
> im Gegenteil: sie wehrt sich gegen das Ungeg-
> liederte durch Schaffung von Gegliedertem.
> Jede künsterlische Tat ist ein Akt der Ver-
> teidigung, der Selbstbehauptung, der Abwehr
> des Tödlichen (innerhalb der menschlichen
> Grenzen).(57)

The creative act, then, is a form of defence which helps to assert human values when they seem threatened by the indifference of the rest of the universe. In addition, Usinger seeks through his poems to transform the awesomeness of infinity and to lend a new significance to what exists outside the earth:

> Laß
> Die Sonnen und Planeten, die
> Nicht singen können,
> Im tiefen Grunde deiner Gesänge
> Mitsingen.(58)

Through the medium of his poetry Usinger is enabled to bestow upon the planets a quality which they do not possess, a voice, the power to communicate. Poetry can penetrate beyond the superficial aspects of life to the 'ewiges Bild' or 'das angedeutete Himmlische' (59) contained in all life:

> Im Reich der Gesänge ist es gewaltiger noch
> Als auf Erden.
> Denn alles ist dort reiner und mehr es selbst.
> Das Helle ist heller, das Heitere heiterer

Und das Grausame grausamer.(60)

This 'condensation' of reality enables man to see more clearly the true nature of each earthly phenomenon, un-clouded by the immediate concerns of everyday life. Especially within the context of a technological society, poetry has a crucial function to perform, and can aspire towards the basic truths more than science can ever hope to do: 'Die Wissenschaften sind notwendigerweise spezia-lisiert, die Dichtung ist die Bemühung um das Gesamte, um das Ganze'.(61)

It is evident that one predominant notion which Usinger's vision of the vast cosmos inspires within him is a new awareness of the unique qualities of the planet which is man's home. In Die Verwandlungen he remarks upon the unique fertility of the earth amongst the other planets:

> Als die amerikanischen Astronauten von Monde aus
> die Erde sahen, da war, ... auf dem samtschwarzen
> Raumhintergrund, ein saphirblauer, wie ein Edel-
> stein leuchtender Wasserball. Unter all den
> wüstenhaften, ruinhaften Sonnenplaneten war die
> Erde wie eine Zuflucht allen Lebens ... und darum
> konnte er in einer Farbe leuchten ... in einem
> tiefgetönten, reinen, himmlischen Saphirblau,
> über das zart-weiße Wolkenschleier ziehen.(62)

The earth has the potential of being a 'Stern des Glücks', a 'Juwel des Himmels', particularly since man has been granted the perception and the intelligence to devise means of achieving this end. In Der Planet too Usinger refers to the earth as a 'Glücksgestirn'(63) and in Die himmlische Heimkehr as 'der selige Planet'. Although the earth is adrift somewhere in the vast cosmos and not the centre of the universe, yet it appears to support forms of life unique in the solar system. It is from the earth too that love originates and wings its way out into the depths of the cosmos:

> der selige Planet,
> Der seine Wandelwege geht
> Und der aus Kraft, die ihn verleibt,
> Das Liebe-Wort ins Weltall schreibt.(64)

Usinger therefore exhorts man to make every effort to fulfil the potential of the earth and utilise its resources,
together with his own, to create order and beauty:

> Unsere menschliche Aufgabe ist es, deshalb, mög-
> lichst viel Ordnung zu stiften. Die Morphologie
> der Erde verpflichtet uns sozusagen zu einem klas-
> sischen Prinzip in unseren äußeren und inneren
> Lebensformen, also auch in der Kunst.(65)

By the 'klassischer Prinzip' Usinger means not an abstract
classicism acted out by idealised figures, which ignores
the undesirable elements of human nature and of the world
in general, but one founded upon reality, on natural forms
as they exist. This new mode of classicism he regards
as a suitable substitute for metaphysical belief, since
it channels man's religious spirit towards earthly things.
Once man has attained greater awareness of the fact that
creation follows an ordered pattern, he can then apply
this knowledge to his own life and organise his own
thoughts and actions in a positive manner.

Man's chief strengths are his mental and emotional
capacities - his intelligence, his imagination, and his
ability to love. With these qualities he could produce
a civilisation and culture which would endure for all
time as a fitting testimony to the unique achievements
of humanity:

> Die Erde ist dein Stern. Mach du ihn leuch-
> > tend,
>
> Ein Juwel des Himmels,
> Weltzeiten lang verkündend, was
> Hier solchen Glanz nach außen wirft:
> Aus Geist eine Galaxis wie
> Aus Diamanten sternenhaft gefügt.(66)

However, instead of exploiting his own potential and that of the earth, man has destroyed all the options propounded by religious teachers or by poets and artists and has become the victim of his own 'Einsichtslosigkeit, Leidenschaft und Besitzgier'. 'Die Menschen schaffen Gewaltiges', writes Usinger, 'und sie zerstören alles wieder, sinnlos, und empfinden noch nicht einmal ein Bedauern darüber'.(67) He sees man's only hope of survival in his being brought to a full awareness of his limitations, and describes man in these terms:

> In unendlichen Weltzusammenhängen ein winziges, bescheidenes Geschöpf, das lernen muß, sich seiner Grenzen bewußt zu werden, wenn er sich nicht völlig vernichten will.(68)

Usinger believes that the basis of human ills resides in man's false conception of his own relative significance which leads him into paths of selfishness and greed. Usinger aspires to replace this outlook with a more productive concept and sees the poet's task as the revelation of what he terms 'die unmittelbare Beziehung Ich-Kosmos',(69) helping man to see his own position in its full context. His own works seek to demonstrate that the validity of earthly things can be reasserted in the face of a disinterested cosmos in such a way that man benefits from the new relationship. The new values which he conceives of are devoid of self-interest: his concept of love extends beyond an actual person; he enjoys the beauty of Nature for its own sake and appreciates it all the more when he considers the barren planets surrounding the earth; and the frustrations of everyday life appear trivial when viewed in the context of the cosmos as a whole. In the words of Hagen:

> Das Hiesige ist im Bewußtsein des Ganzen gesehen. Das Nahe verliert seine Enge und Privatheit, das Ferne seine Schrecken. Der Mensch lebt nicht mehr zufällig und im Beziehungslosen.(70)

From the despondency caused by the prospect of the end-
less void around the earth, which appears to destroy the
significance of human actions, Usinger progresses to a
more optimistic stance. Although the 'Ich-Kosmos' situation can never be satisfactorily resolved since man's
senses and mental faculties are inadequate to a total
comprehension of anything so vast and diverse as the universe, Usinger believes that once the reality of man's
situation in the cosmos has been recognised, a true
appreciation of the most valuable aspects of human life
can then result in the cultivation of a new creative and
meaningful existence for mankind.

NOTES

1. Usinger, _Tellurium_, pp.137-8.
2. M. Butor, _SF: The other side of realism_, p.164.
3. Usinger, _Tellurium_, pp.144-5.
4. _Alfred Mombert. Ausstellung zum 25. Todestag_,
   Karlsruhe, 1967, p.13.
5. Usinger, _Tellurium_, p.144.
6. ibid.
7. Usinger, _Der ewige Kampf_, p.35.
8. Usinger, _Geist und Gestalt_, p.147.
9. ibid.
10. Usinger, _Geist und Gestalt_, p.148.
11. Usinger, _Merkbücher_, p.7.
12. Usinger, _Merkbücher_, p.30.
13. Usinger, _Merkbücher_, p.12.
14. Usinger, _Hermes_, p.14.
15. Usinger, _Niemandsgesang_, p.15.
16. _Der Dichter Fritz Usinger spricht über sein Werk._
    (Tonbandaufnahme vom 3.6.1971 durch Herbert Lehmitz),
    see C. R. Barker, 'Fritz Usinger: Poet, Essayist and
    Critic', p.644.
17. Hagen, op. cit., p.77.
18. Pascal, _Pensées et Opuscules_, ed. L. Brunschvieg,
    Paris, 1967, p.350.

19. Usinger, <u>Niemandsgesang</u>, p.20.
20. Usinger, <u>Niemandsgesang</u>, p.21.
21. Usinger, <u>Canopus</u>, p.10.
22. Usinger, <u>Canopus</u>, pp.10-11.
23. Usinger, <u>Niemandsgesang</u>, p.27.
24. Usinger, <u>Gedanken</u> (1960) unpaginated. (Reprinted in <u>Merkbücher</u>, p.20)
25. Usinger, <u>Der Stern Vergeblichkeit</u>, p.90.
26. Usinger, <u>Der Sinn und das Sinnlose</u> (1970), unpaginated.
27. Usinger, <u>Der Stern Vergeblichkeit</u>, p.46.
28. Usinger, <u>Niemandsgesang</u>, p.18.
29. Usinger, <u>Der Stern Vergeblichkeit</u>, p.71.
30. Usinger, <u>Der Stern Vergeblichkeit</u>, p.90.
31. Usinger, <u>Canopus</u>, p.33.
32. Usinger, <u>Der Stern Vergeblichkeit</u>, p.91.
33. Usinger, <u>Canopus</u>, p.39.
34. Letter 20 (10.11.71).
35. Usinger, <u>Die himmlische Heimkehr</u>, 'Liebe-Wort'. (Since this volume is still in manuscript form at the time of writing, references are to poem titles.)
36. Usinger, <u>Canopus</u>, p.54.
37. ibid.
38. Usinger, <u>Der Sinn und das Sinnlose</u>.
39. Usinger, <u>Die himmlische Heimkehr</u>, 'Die Grenze'.
40. Usinger, <u>Canopus</u>, p.55.
41. Usinger, <u>Der Sinn und das Sinnlose</u>.
42. Usinger, <u>Der Planet</u>, p.77.
43. Usinger, <u>Der Sinn und das Sinnlose</u>. (Reprinted in <u>Merkbücher</u>, p.45).
44. Usinger, <u>Das Wirkliche</u>, p.151.
45. Usinger, <u>Die himmlische Heimkehr</u>, 'Huldigung für Dante II'.
46. Usinger, <u>Die himmlische Heimkehr</u>, 'Huldiging für Dante III'.
47. Usinger, <u>Die himmlische Heimkehr</u>, 'Die Grenze'.
48. Usinger, <u>Die himmlische Heimkehr</u>, 'Das Labyrinth'.
49. Usinger, <u>Die himmlische Heimkehr</u>, 'Der Zeit-Dom'.
50. Usinger, <u>Die himmlische Heimkehr</u>, 'Himmlischer

Wirbel'.
51. Usinger, Die himmlische Heimkehr, 'Das Labyrinth'.
52. Usinger, Galaxis, p.72.
53. Usinger, Die himmlische Heimkehr, 'Die Welten-Fuge'.
54. Usinger, Die himmlische Heimkehr, 'Die Welten-Fuge'.
55. Letter 28.4.76.
56. Letter 28.4.76.
57. Letter 10.6.76.
58. Usinger, Die himmlische Heimkehr, 'Die große Umkehr'.
59. Usinger, Der Stern Vergeblichkeit, p.79.
60. Usinger, Der Stern Vergeblichkeit, p.87.
61. Usinger, Welt ohne Klassik, p.52.
62. Usinger, Die Verwandlungen, p.70.
63. Usinger, Der Planet, p.105.
64. Usinger, Die himmlische Heimkehr, 'Liebe-Wort'.
65. Letter 31.5.76.
66. Usinger, Die himmlische Heimkehr, 'Die große Umkehr'.
67. Usinger, Die Verwandlungen, p.71.
68. Usinger, Welt ohne Klassik, p.70.
69. Letter 6 (16.11.69).
70. Hagen, op. cit., p.261.

CONCLUSION

Throughout his life, Usinger has dedicated himself to
a search for an elusive truth. One of the principal features of this long and patient search is humility, in
the sense that Usinger does not sugggest that man should
take over the world after the 'death of God' but, on the
contrary, that man should face the realities of his situation and rest content with a relatively subordinate role
in the cosmos. Usinger acknowledges that this recognition can readily inspire fear and insecurity, but he
welcomes a confrontation with even the most awesome aspects
of man's new situation. A remarkable feature of Usinger's
work is that pessimism is never permitted to dominate.
He knows that he will never hold the key to the mysteries
of the cosmos, but despite that it is the search which is
crucial.

It is fundamental to Usinger's conception of a quest
or search that he dedicates himself utterly to it, obli-
vious of trends and fashions in literature and philosophy.
He is especially antipathetical towards a concern with the
seemingly 'relevant' areas of experience such as social
problems and politics. Instead, he concerns himself with
the enduring and fundamental issues of man in an infinite
cosmos. He is fully aware that in so doing he is working
against the predominant tendencies of the human psyche,
which is constantly preoccupied with its immediate surroundings:

> Dein kleines irdisches Reich, das Hin und Her,
> Das Nahe, Eingeschränkte,
> Das Tun ohne Aufblick und Fernblick.
> Ich lud dich ein in eine Welt der Weite.(1)

His life's work has now come full circle, as he explains
in a recent letter:

> Erde, Weltall, Blick in die Unendlichkeit, Umkehr
> im Weltall, Rückkehr zur Erde. Nur von diesem
> astronautischen Geist-Flug aus sind die Zusammen-

hänge meiner Bücher zu verstehen. (2)

The restricted, anthropocentric viewpoint of Usinger's early poems is far removed from the penetrating vision of his 'Rückkehr zur Erde' in his latest collection Die himmlische Heimkehr. It is significant that this new publication follows rapidly upon the heels of Galaxis, which explores the darker regions of the cosmos. Unlike those politicians who portray the gloom yet offer no solution, Usinger is unwilling to leave man abandoned in the void and seeks to show how earthly life can be lived according to a new set of values determined by its significance within the cosmos as a whole.

The penalty which Usinger has paid for his single-minded dedication to the task he set himself is that he has been ignored by the reading public at large, who seek inspiration in socially-orientated literature and are reluctant to consider fundamental issues of any kind. This clearly is a source of regret to Usinger, as many of his poems reveal:

> Es ist Zeit, daß ihr mich vergeßt.
> Was ich tat, war zu wenig,
> Als daß ihr meiner gedenken könntet.
> Ich war keine Welt.
> Ich war nur ein Mund der Welt.
> Viele ihrer Geheimnisse wußte ich,
> Und ich sagte sie, deutlich, genau.
> Niemand hörte hin.
> Alle waren zu beschäftigt. (3)

These lines express the pain which his neglect has caused him. Usinger's sense of injustice has of necessity been increased by the success of inferior writers, for his own poetry is technically of a high order. Essentially a traditionalist, he demonstrates his mastery of a wide range of poetic forms, such as the sonnet, acrostic and sestina, by adapting them to his own ends. He has in latter years developed a characteristic style of his own, employing free verse whose flowing rhythms dis-

guise the difficulties of this form. The style of his
poems is always adapted to suit their subject-matter;
for example, it was noted in the previous chapter that
many of them have cyclical tendencies associated with
his cosmological outlook. Recurrent themes and varia-
tions occur both within individual poems and from one
volume to the next, as Usinger explores the multitude
of interrelated forces which together form a cosmic
unity.

Nor are Usinger's activities and skill confined to
the realm of poetry. Essays, critical studies and
aphorisms introduce further variety of forms as Usinger
explores a wide range of subjects, such as mythology,
cosmology, mysticism and alchemy, where Usinger's lifelong quest can be compared to the alchemists' search
for the Philosophers' Stone. He also examines new
approaches to traditional themes; for example, he relates mythos and logos, maintaining that the Logos
itself is a kind of 'myth' since it represents a metaphysical concept which man is unable to define with any
degree of precision. Once he has assimilated all the
traditional modes of thought with which he is confronted, Usinger sets out to express them in terms of his
own world of imagery. He gives new meanings to traditional figures of mythology, and invents his own 'späte
Nymphe'. He builds up a complex of imagery which corresponds to his basic preoccupations: his 'niemand',
which expresses a sense of the cosmic void; his concept
of 'Vergeblichkeit' as a positive notion; his 'Engel
der Vergessenheit', which brings consolation to man;
and images such as the organ, or the sounds of Nature
which offer insight into the core of the universe.
Usinger compounds all these elements into his own philosophy which, despite its enormous range, is remarkable for its unity and consistency.

NOTES

1. Usinger, Der Stern Vergeblichkeit, p.68.

2. Letter 10.6.76.
3. Usinger, <u>Canopus</u>, p.50.

SELECT BIBLIOGRAPHY

(For a complete listing of Usinger's works see W. H. Braun,
'Bibliographie Fritz Usinger' in S. Hagen (ed.), Die Götter
lesen nicht, Bonn, 1975, pp.177-245; and for a more comprehensive account of the secondary literature see C. R. Barker,
'Fritz Usinger: Poet, Essayist and Critic', Ph.D., Hull,
1975, pp.661-663.)

A. Primary Works

1. Poetry

Der ewige Kampf, Darmstadt, 1918.
Große Elegie, Darmstadt, 1920.
Irdisches Gedicht, Darmstadt, 1927.
Sonette, Bad Nauheim, 1927.
Das Wort, Darmstadt, 1931.
Die Stimmen, Darmstadt, 1934.
Die Geheimnisse, Darmstadt, 1937.
Gedichte (Auswahl), Hamlin, 1940.
Hermes, Darmstadt, 1942.
Traum der Erde, Hamburg, 1942.
Das Glück, Darmstadt, 1947.
Hesperische Hymnen, Stuttgart, 1948.
Veilchen, Offenbach a.M., 1950.
Gesang gegen den Tod, Frankfurt a.M., 1952.
Fest der Geister, Heidelberg, 1955.
Niemandgesang, Offenbach a.M., 1957.
Der Morgenstern, Wuppertal, 1957.
Der Stern Vergeblichkeit, Munich, 1962.
Pentagramm, Wiesbaden, 1965.
Krokus-Gesang, Offenbach a.M., 1965.
Canopus, Wiesbaden, 1968.
Der Planet, Darmstadt, 1972.
Galaxis, Offenbach a.M., 1975.
Die himmlische Heimkehr, in press.

2. Essays

Geist und Gestalt, Darmstadt, 1939.
Medusa, Dessau, 1940.
Das Wirkliche, Darmstadt, 1947.

Zur Metaphysik des Clowns, Offenbach a.M., 1952.
Dank an die Mutter, Offenbach a.M., 1952.
Kleine Biographie des Jazz, Offenbach a.M., 1953.
Friedrich Schiller und die Idee des Schönen, Wiesbaden, 1955.
Form und Wahrheit der zeitgenössischen Literatur, Wiesbaden, 1955.
Über den Abschied, Munich, 1956.
Das grüne Sofa, Offenbach a.M., 1956.
Walt Whitman, Wiesbaden, 1957.
Edgar Allan Poe, Darmstadt, 1959.
Stefan George und die Gegenwart, Darmstadt, 1960.
Welt ohne Klassik, Darmstadt, 1960.
Ernst Wilhelm Nay, Recklinghausen, 1961.
Tellurische und planetarische Dichtung, Wiesbaden, 1963.
Die geistige Figur des Clowns in unserer Zeit, Wiesbaden, 1964.
Gesichter und Gesichte, Darmstadt, 1965.
Das Ungeheuer Sprache, Darmstadt, 1965.
Die dichterische Welt Hans Arp, Wiesbaden, 1965.
Die Lahn (Fotoband mit Einleitung), Königstein im Taunus, 1965.
Der Spessart (Fotoband mit Einleitung), Königstein im Taunus, 1965.
Hessen im Farbbild (mit Begleittexten), Frankfurt a.M., 1966.
Tellurium, Neuwied, 1966.
Gottfried Benn und die Medizin, Wiesbaden, 1967.
Das unwahrscheinliche Glück, Olten, 1969.
Dichtung als Information, Mainz, 1970.
Die Verwandlungen, Mainz, 1971.
Haus aus Kubus und Kugel, Darmstadt, 1971.
Wissenschaft und Dichtung, Mainz, 1974.

3. Aphorisms

Gedanken, Wuppertal, 1959.
Notizbuch, Darmstadt, 1966.
Der Sinn und das Sinnlose, Darmstadt, 1970.
Merkbücher, Mainz, 1976.

B. Secondary Literature

G. Bäumer, Der Dichter Fritz Usinger, Tübingen, 1947.
H. A. Seelbach, Dichtung und Weltbild Fritz Usingers,
Bad Nauheim, 1948.
E. Schmahl, Fritz Usinger, Tradition und Wagnis, Friedberg,
1951.
A. Braun, Weltträger, Friedberg, 1965.
K. Krolowm, Laudatio auf Fritz Usinger, printed privately.
A. Braun, Große und Trauer des Worts, Gießen, 1970.
S. Hagen, Fritz Usinger, Endlichkeit und Unendlichkeit,
Bonn, 1972.
C. R. Barker, 'Fritz Usinger: Poet, Essayist and Critic',
Ph.D., Hull, 1975.
S. Hagen (ed), Die Götter lesen nicht. Fritz Usinger zum
80. Geburtstag am 5. März 1975, Bonn, 1975.
E. R. Niederhöff, Fritz Usinger, Friedberg, 1975.